Sinister Wisdom 136
Spring 2025

Publisher: Sinister Wisdom, Inc.
Editor & Publisher: Julie R. Enszer
Managing Editor: Shawn(ta) Smith-Cruz
Assistant Editor: Chloe Weber
Graphic Designer: Nieves Guerra

Board of Directors: Pelaya Arapakis, Chloe Berger, Cheryl Clarke, Julie R. Enszer, Sara Youngblood Gregory, Yeva Johnson, Briona Jones, Judith Katz, Shromona Mandal, Joan Nestle, Rose Norman, Bell Pitkin, Mecca Jamilah Sullivan, Yasmin Tambiah, Darla Tejada, and Li-Anne Wright.

Cover artwork: Street Scene
Artist Name: Kinga Stefaniec
Media: Photograph
Artist Bio: Queer anarchist Thin White Dyke born in 1980 in Poland. In 2010 achieving diploma in Polish study in Silesian University.

Kinga Stefaniec Publications:
Nuthouse Episode 2018 poetry collection discontinued debut novel published under pen name Aleks Koval Explosives Under Special Supervision which was banned by Bristol Book Club for Women as too controversial.

City & Mind Coda published in 2020.

Grazing the wallpaper of Reality in 2022.

Artwork exhibited in Southbank Centre in London received Koestler Awards in multi cathegory on international exhibition 2015 -2018.

Cooperate with PRSC art club.

Writes and lives in Bristol in United Kingadom.

See cover artist statement on page 201.

CONTENTS

NOTES FOR A MAGAZINE

Who are your icons? When did you first encounter them? What effect have these icons had on your life? Icons, both people and objects, experiences, and memories, are important; they define elements of what we value, of what is important to us culturally, of what we deem worthy of care, attention, and veneration.

This issue of *Sinister Wisdom*, *Sinister Wisdom* 136: *Icons*, considers a range of lesbian, feminist, and queer icons. *Sinister Wisdom* 136: *Icons* builds on two contemporary strengths of Sinister Wisdom: excavating the lesbian-feminist past in meaningful present-day contexts and profiling amazing new lesbian writing.

Sinister Wisdom 136: *Icons* opens with a series of portraits by visual artist L.A. "Happy" Hyder of Audre Lorde. Lorde's iconic status beyond lesbian and feminist communities continues to delight me even as I am amazed by her travels beyond our communities. These photographs remind me of the ways that Lorde nurtured our communities and how we nurtured her. The best iconic relationships are mutual, reciprocal, and build power and joy. Thank you to Happy Hyder for entrusting *Sinister Wisdom* with this work.

The animating impulse for *Sinister Wisdom* 136: *Icons* came from Susan Sherman and my interest in thinking about the feminist journal *IKON* that she edited. Sinister Wisdom continues to be interested in the feminist and lesbian work of the women in print movement from the 1970s, 1980s, and 1990s. After the Lorde photographs, there is a dossier of work about *IKON* that includes a wonderful essay by Susan Sherman about her work with *IKON* followed by four reflections about its work and influence. This dossier concludes with three poems by Susan Sherman, a powerful and important poet.

Sinister Wisdom 136: *Icons* features a robust selection of new lesbian writing, bringing new and returning voices to these pages. This work is followed by a section with articles about lesbian pulps.

At our fall 2024 fundraising event, Night of a Thousand Lesbian Feminist Queer Voices, Katherine V. Forrest read movingly from *Lesbian Pulp Fiction*, a book she edited about twenty years ago for Cleis Press; as Katherine noted that evening, the writers of pulp remind us we are never going back no matter what challenges face us now or in the future. Lesbian pulps are a well to which we (lesbians and folks interested in thinking about lesbians) return for inspiration. I am grateful to all these authors for revisiting this work anew.

Sinister Wisdom 136: *Icons* concludes with an oral history by Dartricia Rollins of Linda Bryant one of the founders of Charis Books and More which celebrated their fiftieth anniversary in the fall of 2024. There are many wonderful pieces to discover in this issue. I hope that you enjoy them all.

While there are many icons in these pages, I want to emphasize that we as a community—in the myriad ways we define that word—select and promote our own icons. Different times, different places, different politics invite new and different icons to represent who we are. Collectively, we all engage in the work of creating icons, in the joy curating a shared culture, and in promoting icons to ourselves and to the world. Thank you for being part of this co-creation with *Sinister Wisdom*.

Julie R. Enszer, PhD
April 2025

PHOTOGRAPHING AUDRE LORDE

L. A. Hyder

I came into the Lesbian Community and the San Francisco Women's Building Community fully formed and yet thoroughly unformed. Newly moved a block away from the newly opened Women's Building on 18ᵗʰ Street in the Mission, I attended a community meeting to discuss an awarded art grant.

Many responded to a call put out on flyers sent to the mailing list and posted around the Bay Area. A few ideas were considered; an art gallery was chosen and given space on the top floor. A small group met, chose our name, and the Vida Gallery Collective was born. This is where I began my long association with arts management and cut my teeth on exhibiting my work personally and learning a gallery's needs.

A few months into planning, Wendy Cadden joined the collective. With Wendy came connections to the Lesbian world of art and writing and a benefit poetry reading for the gallery by Audre Lorde. I'd heard a few of Audre's taped readings on our local radio station and read her poetry and pieces of her about to be released book, *Zami: A new spelling of my name*, in various publications like *Sinister Wisdom* and *Connections*.

And then I was face to face with Audre Lorde, who said, "Ah, now I know why they call you Happy!," and we embraced.

When *Zami* was released, I rushed to Old Wives' Tales bookstore, a successful collective effort on Valencia Street, and scooped up my copy. I also purchased Maureen Brady's *Folly*, just out, and a book I'd followed through those same publications. What a joyous Dyke moment!

A year or so later, Audre and Pat Parker gave a reading at the Women's Building.

I arrived just as the reading began, having gone with a friend to the Ashram in Oakland. At the end of the Guru's talk, it was customary for everyone to get in line (new attendees first) and as you stand before her, receive a hug. Wanting to get to the reading at the Women's Building, I left before my hug.

Arriving, I saw a group at the front of the hall near the stage. As I got to the group, they parted and there was Audre. As I walked toward her, she asked how my art was going, then embraced me. She was my blessing that night.

Audre was reading at the University of California a few days later. I asked to photograph her. She said yes.

These are a few of the images taken that day in Wendy's back yard.

Although my face-to-face time with Audre was minimal, her impact on my senses remains maximal.

The early 1980s were a time of portraits. I was fortunate to
meet Alice Walker when she needed a portrait for
The Color Purple book jacket

Etel Adnan, Lebanese poet, painter and philosopher, used
this portrait for an exhibit of her work in Washington, DC

The Vida Gallery Collective,
in our third floor space in the
San Francisco Women's Building.

TRIBUTE TO *IKON*

CREATIVITY AND CHANGE:
IKON, THE SECOND SERIES

Susan Sherman

After months of work and preparation, the launch of the Second Series of *IKON* was actually about to happen. I was busy gathering the names of the readers still missing as the last of the overflow crowd streamed into the auditorium from the large waiting area at the NYU Law School—the auditorium had been made available to us thanks to co-sponsorship by NYU Law Women. I was simultaneously excited, apprehensive, delighted. First issue contributors to the magazine were gathered in the front two rows of the auditorium. Seated beside me were Audre Lorde and Hettie Jones, Jewelle Gomez, Lois Elaine Griffith, Davine, Akua Lezli Hope, Patricia Jones, Rachel deVries, Blanche Wiesen Cook, Michelle Cliff, Irena Klepfisz and Jan Clausen.

Finally, everything was in place. It was October 16, 1982, and *IKON* magazine was about to be reborn as a feminist/activist journal staffed by women, celebrating work by women. The Second Series of *IKON* was an organic extension of the original affirmation of *IKON* from the first series. The slogan *Creativity and Change* was carried over, along with a slogan taken from the cover of a Tri-Continental magazine I brought back when I returned in 1968 from the Cultural Congress of Havana. The original cover was a map of the world that could be cut out and formed into a new shape. We adapted the cover from the first series of *IKON*, and it would serve as the guiding motto: *"We can and must create a new world with new forms, techniques and ideas."*

Creativity and Change was already a permanent part of our logo and it, along with a short essay of Audre Lorde's, "Poetry is Not a Luxury," had served as the inspiration to publish *IKON* again. In her essay, Lorde characterizes poetry "as illumination... as a vital necessity of our existence....the way we help give name to the name-less so it can be thought..." (*IKON* Second Series #1, pg.36)

Born in 1939, I grew up during World War II. Nighttime was punctuated by the sound of air raid sirens as we rushed to drape dark curtains over the windows, just in case, and morning dawned with soldiers singing, marching to the nearby naval base two blocks from where my mother worked as a salesperson at a liquor store. What I remember from those early years was hearing what seemed like endless horror stories of the holocaust and how lucky we were that my grandparents had emigrated. I was also simulta-neously transfixed and terrified as my family gathered around the radio, listening to accounts of the dropping of the atomic bomb. My earliest memories were of prejudice, violence and injustice.

In third grade, I created, edited and wrote my first poems and collected stories for a little hand-made magazine. In High School, journalism classes meant working on the high school newspaper soliciting and editing content, designing layouts, and every Thurs-day, in the type-shop (they used metal linotype in those days), locking up the metal lines of type for proof sheets, until the final product was distributed on Monday morning.

So I was not totally unprepared in 1966, when Arthur Sainer, a playwright and theater critic for the Village Voice, and his friend, Thomas Muth, who generously donated $1500 for seed money, got together with Nancy Colin, an artist, and myself to discuss put-ting out a new magazine. I was to be the book and theater critic and Nancy was to design the first issue. It was her idea to integrate graphics and words, one of the hallmarks of *IKON*. After a year of meetings with no actual magazine, I finally said I would make sure the magazine came out, but I had to be the editor. They agreed, and *IKON* was born. After the first issue, Arthur and Tom dropped out; Nancy and I were on our own.

We decided on *IKON* as the name for the new journal (the K because Nancy felt it worked into graphic design better). For us, the word *IKON* symbolized synthesis—words and pictures, art and politics, creativity and change, the separate parts fused as one into an organic unity in which all the parts could be perceived simultaneously, the way you perceive a picture. We believed there was no conflict between theory and art, art and action, that "there was no place for the middleman," that artists were perfectly capable of understanding and writing about their own and other artists' work—anyone who has ever read the letters of Van Gogh, the Blue Rider edited by Kandinsky, one could go on endlessly, should have understood that. But the Fifties and Sixties, according to Academia, was the age of the critic, not the artist, of analysis, not originality.

As the first series of *IKON* progressed, so did its political content, centered squarely on the epic events, both political and cultural, of the Sixties. In those years, I made two trips to Cuba. In 1969, with the first series *IKON* #6 devoted to the Cultural Congress of Havana, our distributors simultaneously "mysteriously" decided to drop the magazine, sending it back undistributed. Our circulation was over 8,000 copies, the format and distribution geared toward newsstand sales. We published one more issue, but it was the end of *IKON*: the major source of our income had been cut off. On principal, during the Vietnam War, we had refused governmental money of any kind. We continued the spirit of *IKON* until 1971 with *IKON*books, a bookstore that sold very few books but became a counter-culture political and cultural center. But the pressure had taken its toll on me—I had lost my job and lived through months of illness—and it just became impossible to continue.

In 1982, my stepfather died and left me $5000. I decided to revive *IKON*, which had been so abruptly shut down in the Sixties, keeping the same name. After much thought, I decided to start with numbering the new series, *IKON* Second Series 1, to avoid the confusion if it had started with #8 from the first series.

In the intervening years between the original *IKON* and the Second Series, I had also become actively involved in the women's movement and had come out as a lesbian—even though I had been involved exclusively in relationships with women since the early Sixties. It was important to me that this new *IKON* reaffirmed that identity rather than subsuming it or actively hiding it as I felt I had to during those difficult early years. This new *IKON* would be staffed by women, published by women, celebrating women's work.

After the first issue, we incorporated as non-profit, got our charities registration number, and received some funding from the literature division of NYSCA (the New York State Council on the Arts), which was headed at the time by Gregory Kolovakos, a creative, progressive young gay man who died of AIDS in 1990. The money from NYSCA, along with money from subscriptions and contributions (including my salary) and all the work being done on a volunteer basis, allowed us to continue publishing. We tried to pay contributors whenever we could, even if only a small fee.

This series of *IKON*, in every sense of the word, was a collaboration. Besides the issues done with organizations, over the years of publication many remarkably talented women contributed as staff members, editors of fiction and poetry, photographers, lay-out artists and designers. This second iteration of the journal ran from 1982 to 1994—twelve magazines, now all book length, averaging around 140 pages, including three double issues, in total almost 2000 pages. The 7x9 non-standard dimension of the magazine was chosen because of the importance we gave to artwork. Each issue of *IKON* was centered loosely on a different theme, either carrying through the entire issue or as a special section.

The premier issue of the second series, *IKON* 1, besides Margaret Randall's photos, featured the first published short story of Jewelle Gomez, poems by Cherríe Moraga and Judith Malina as well as the poets already listed who read at the inaugural reading; as well as the work of Mercè Rodoreda, a Catalan writer translated by David Rosenthal. Suzanne Lacy wrote an analysis of a performance she did with Leslie Labowitz, "In Mourning and in Rage," which was inspired by the activism of Women Against Violence Against Women (WAVAW). Candace Lyle Hogan interviewed Blanche Wiesen Cook. Margaret was also the Contributing Editor. This first issue would be an indication of the breadth of work that *IKON* would publish in the years to come.

IKON 2 opened with a portfolio of photographs, "City Children," by Colleen McKay. We actually started the portfolio on the front cover. The inside front cover became the title page, and the photos then led directly from the cover photo into the table of contents, in keeping with our attempt to make both the placement and the choice of visual material as creative as possible. Next to the photo on the cover was a favorite quote from H.D.—"We Are More Than We Know."

Lynette Hirschman, who was working on computer languages at NYU, was my roommate for a number of months in the Eighties. I was also, at the time, working on an article called "The Tyranny of Form" based on a critique of the work of Marshall McLuhan, and between us, we came up with the idea of making the special section of Issue 2, *Women and the Computer*. It would center on "The New Technology's Effects On Our Work, On Our Lives." Computerization was just beginning to be discussed, and the two words "women" and "computer" were seldom, if ever, seen together. Included in the special section were essays on theory, on graphics, a Technology Information Sheet, and Molly Jackson and Toni Russell, two computer repairwomen, wrote about the effects of technology on the workplace.

Poets, writers, and artists represented in the issue included Paula Gunn Allen, Judith McDaniel, with excerpts from their new novels; prose by Beth Brant, Alexis de Veaux and Luisa Valenzuela; music by Patsy Rogers; the artwork of Bea Kreloff; photography by Colleen McKay and Margaret Randall, and poetry by Fay Chiang, Cheryl Clark, June Jordan, Martha King, and Susan Saxe. Myriam Díaz-Diocaretz joined Margaret Randall as a contributing editor, and Colleen McKay was the staff photographer. Janet Newell typeset the entire issue in the days before computer typesetting.

IKON 3 (Spring/Summer 1984) had a special section devoted to *Women in Struggle: Seneca, Medgar Evers, Nicaragua.* They seemed three disparate events, but the tie-in was the focus on women's leadership in the struggle for social justice. Andrée Nicola-McLaughlin, Medgar Evers College's first woman Dean of Administration and spokesperson for the Student-Faculty-Community-Alumni Coalition, spoke about their struggle in an interview by Andrea Doremus, a struggle which would eventually lead to the ouster of the college president. At the time, Medgar Evers College in Brooklyn had a student body that was 95% Black and 75% women, and yet only three appointments out of twenty in Deanships were women, and there were no courses about Black women.

The Seneca Women's Encampment for a Future of Peace and Justice in front of the Seneca Army Depot was documented in words by Ynestra King, one of the protest's leading activists, and by Catherine Allport in photographs. One of the obvious reasons for the site being chosen as a women's action was because in 1848, the American feminist movement formally began in Seneca, New York. But a more pressing reason in 1984 was that the

Seneca Army Depot was a storage site for cruise missiles slated to be shipped to Europe. Allport's photo documentation includes graphic photos of police arresting the women, but perhaps the most moving photo is one of the group empowered by their solidarity. We realized with this issue how *IKON* could be used as a vehicle for presenting women's creative work in the arts while at the same time documenting feminist activism.

The section on Nicaragua included an essay, "Feminism and the Nicaraguan Revolution," written as a result of my trip to the Conference on Central America in 1983. It was accompanied by photographs by Colleen McKay. Margaret Randall's interview with Nicaraguan poet, Vidaluz Meneses, "We Cannot Talk about the Revolution in the Third Person," was accompanied by two of Meneses' poems, printed both in Spanish and the English translation by Margaret, a practice we would continue with bilingual material in subsequent issues. It also included a portfolio of drawings by Margo Machida based on her experience as a psychiatric aide.

To coincide with the launch of Issue #3, *IKON* sponsored an event at PS 41, a public grammar school, with presentations by Dr. Zala Chandler, a leader of the struggle at Medgar Evers, and Adrienne Rich, who spoke about the trip we had taken to Nicaragua for the conference. A videotape was shown of the arrests of the women from Seneca. Kimiko Hahn, whom I met at the conference and who would become a friend and an important part of *IKON*, read her poetry. There were also women from the special U.S. tour of "Guatemalan Women Speak" and a representative from AMES (Asociacion de Mujeres de El Salvador). Davine, who joined *IKON* as Associate Editor, MCed the event, and we welcomed Beth Brant as a Contributing Editor. Ellen Turner took the lead in designing the issue, a task she would assume for many future issues.

A theme of *IKON* 4 (Winter/Summer 1985) was *Women and Photography*. This time, instead of a special section, portfolios of photographs were interspersed in the issue. It was our general policy to print portfolios of artwork rather than scattering featured artists' and photographers' work throughout the magazine to more fully represent them and not present their work as an interlude or illustration. The photographers represented were Maria Theriza Alves, "Recovering My History: Butia, Brazil: A Journal in Photos and Words" as well as portfolios by Edna Bennett, Colleen McKay, Marisela La Grave and Margaret Randall. The issue also included among its many contributors excerpts from longer works by Beth Brant, Judy Grahn and Judith McDaniel, as well as prose and poems by Meena Alexander, Gloria Anzaldúa, Enid Dame, Kathy Engel, Suzanne Gardinier, Janice Gould, Marilyn Hacker, Audre Lorde, Minnie Bruce Pratt and Nellie Wong.

With *IKON* 5/6 (Winter/Summer 1986), *Art Against Apartheid: Works for Freedom*, we began publishing special double issues that could also be sold as books. This issue was the first that we did in collaboration with a collective. It grew out of a combined reading *IKON* did with the Art Against Apartheid Committee, a group of artists and writers actively working against Apartheid in South Africa. Gale Jackson from Art Against Apartheid and I were the co-ordinating editors. Besides contributing part of the content, *IKON* was responsible for the final "putting together" and publication of the issue, as well as publicity and distribution. It was certainly our most ambitious project. Major funding for the issue came from the United Nations Special Committee Against Apartheid, with Major-General Joseph N. Garba (CFR), the committee's chairman of the committee, writing an introductory statement of support. The rest of the funding came from readers' contributions of readers and a grant from the New York State Council for the Arts. Alice Walker wrote an introduction to the issue.

Divided into two sections, *South Africans Speak* and *Art Against Apartheid: Works for Freedom,* fifty writers and forty-seven visual artists, women and men, contributed to this issue of *IKON*, which ran 186 pages The cover design was by George "Geo" Smith and the cover art was by Carole Byard.. On the inside front cover, Dennis Brutus, South African poet, educator, activist-in-exile, opened the issue with his poem in honor of South African Freedom Day, June 26, 1967: "...and the mind ranging/wildly as a strayed bird/ seeking some names to settle on/and deeds being done/and those who will do the much/that still needs to be done."

Catherine Allport had just returned from South Africa with a portfolio of photographs; she had also surreptitiously taped leaders of the anti-apartheid movement, some of whom were underground, and after transcribing and editing the tapes, I was able to piece hours of interviews into oral histories that make up the bulk of the section. These included Barbara Masekela, administrative secretary of the ANC Department of Arts and Culture who would later serve as Ambassador to the US from 2003 to 2007 and Albertina Sisulu, president of the United Democratic Front and the cofounder of the Federation of South African women, whose husband, Walter Sisulu, convicted of treason by the apartheid government, was spending twenty-five years in prison alongside Nelson Mandela.

Helen Joseph, another interviewee, was born in England. She was charged with high treason and was the first person to be put under "house arrest" in South Africa. Lastly, there was the "testimony" of an activist white South African whose name had to be withheld. These interviews, along with poems and artwork, make up the remainder of the section, which ends with a long poem/prose poem by Jeremy Cronin, a noted South African poet who served seven years in jail (1976-1983) on charges of terrorism for disseminating propaganda for the ANC and the SACP (South African Communist Party).

The second section of the issue, *Art Against Apartheid: Works for Freedom* tied the issue of South African apartheid with racism in the United States. Nowhere was this stated more succinctly than in Audre Lorde's "Apartheid U.S.A." *Art Against Apartheid: Works for Freedom IKON* 5/6 was formally launched on April 11, 1986, with a reading/celebration at PS 41. *Art Against Apartheid* went into two printings, selling close to 5000 copies. A little more than a year later, at the same venue, we celebrated the return of Margaret Randall to the U.S. and our support for her in her case against deportation with an event that featured her reading and speaking and the music of Casselberry and Dupree.

The theme of *IKON* 7 (Spring/Summer 1987) was *Women and Love*—love in all its manifestations. The title was chosen purposely to make the thematic material as broad as possible. The cover was one of the most striking and, at the same time, the most problematic of any we had done. The design was from a page of artwork from the portfolio "The Meal," by Josely Carvalho, a Brazilian American artist. We decided to experiment with using silver and red inks. It looked beautiful. The problem was the silver ink wasn't stable and easily wiped off. Since we were doing everything ourselves, we learned a lot about the technical issues involved in publishing a magazine. Apart from lay-out and printing, they included fundraising, organizing subscriptions, and all of the business work that would usually be the province of a managing editor. Among others the issue featured an essay by Charlotte Bunch, a play by Clare Coss and work by Meena Alexander, Janice Gould, and Barbara Moraff. Jessica Chapin became an Assistant Editor.

In 1987, *IKON* published a book, *We Stand our Ground: Three Women, Their Vision, Their Poems*, which featured the work of Kimiko Hahn, Gale Jackson and myself—an Asian American poet, an African American poet, and a Jewish Lesbian poet. The cover, as well as the internal design and artwork, was by Josely Carvalho, who had created the art for the cover of the seventh issue. Besides the poetry, the book started with a twenty-page *trialogue*, "Three Voices Together a Collage," the three poets writing about their lives and their theories of activism and writing. It was constructed of questions I wrote, sent to the poets, edited, wove together, and returned to them for their editing and additions. Once the piece was put together, it looked like a seamless "telling." It was later picked up and published in the anthology *Art On The Line: Essays by Artists about the Point where Their Art & Activism Intersect*, edited by Jack Hirschman (Curbstone Press, 2002).

IKON 8 (Winter/Spring 1987-88), was simply called *Journeys*. The range of work here once again is evidenced by the contributors, including work by poets Marjorie Agosín, Karen Brodine, Rachel Guido deVries, Kimiko Hahn, Achy Obejas, Kate Millett; an interview with Joan Larkin by Elly Bulkin; and photography by Claudia Gordilla, an outstanding Nicaraguan photographer. Trix Rosen also contributed a photo journal title "Igorata: The Women of the Cordillera" from the Philippines. Yolanda Blanco took over as Assistant Editor for the issue.

After Issue 8, we did two more issues in collaboration. Our experience with the *Art Against Apartheid* issue had been so positive that we looked for other groups that might need our technical expertise and all-around support. These issues of *IKON* were perhaps the most rewarding because they not only gave us a chance to work collaboratively with activist and artistic collectives but because we felt we were fulfilling a real service by dissemi-

nating important information that came from the women themselves. The creative work was coming *from* them, not from others
writing *about* them.

Asian Women United, "a New York based women's organization
committed to the development of Asian Sisterhood," had already
been working collecting and putting together an anthology when
they got in touch with us to see if we could help them complete
their project. That is how *IKON* 9 (1988), *Without Ceremony*, was
born. Kimiko Hahn acted as the poetry editor, and Penny Fujiko
Willgerodt as the prose coordinator. Lilly Lee designed the issue
and did the cover design. Tomie Arai provided the cover artwork,
as well as contributing a portfolio of work of her own. The Asian
Women United Journal Collective consisted of Sharon Hom,
Debbie Lee, Lily Lee, Susan Louie and Liz Young.

It was the first time another group had almost total control
over the issue and its design, and occasionally, it was frustrating
working with sometimes difficult personalities, but the final re-
ward was an incredible issue including everything from a sexuality
roundtable to a working mother's roundtable, to a veteran political
activists' panel. With fiction by Bharati Mukherjee and Ninotchka
Rosca to an interview with artist Yong Soon Min, with poetry and
prose filling 126 pages, the Collective's anthology was finally realized. *IKON* 9 became a memorable issue, both because in form
and content, it was certainly one of the best and most rewarding
we had published—and because, ironically, it was the project that
lost us our NEA funding.

During the sixties, *IKON* had not been funded by any governmental agency, solely being funded by our salaries and money
from subscriptions and sales. When our distribution at that time
was cut off after my trip to Cuba and our special issue on the Cultural Congress of Havana in 1968, we had no choice but to stop
publishing the magazine. In the eighties, with NEA funding, which
we had received the prior year, plus our continued funding from
the New York State Council on the Arts, it seemed *IKON* could fi-

nally escape constant financial pressure. *IKON* had always tried to pay our contributors, even if it was a small token, when it was at all possible, and had paid some of the layout and design people, but neither the rest of the staff nor I had ever had any kind of monetary recompense for the untold number of hours of work we put into each issue, and I was also looking forward to not having to use my credit card to make up expenses. When we were notified that the magazine had not been funded, it came as a shock. I fully expected that with this remarkable issue *IKON* would continue to receive NEA funding.

During that period, the NEA was under heavy pressure not to fund any Lesbian and Gay material, but naively, I didn't think much about it since we had been publishing Lesbian material for years and *IKON* was well known as an activist magazine, plus there wasn't anything particularly sexually radical in the issue—or at least not to my mind. Since you could call and find out why your funding had been denied, I took advantage of the opportunity to call and see what was up. I was told that future funding had been denied because the writing in the issue was considered "uneven," which came as a surprise to me because *IKON* always published material of the highest caliber, and this issue was one of our best. When I asked for a concrete example, I was told that an article by a woman called Huong Giang Nguyen had been cited. Not remembering exactly what that article was, I hung up and referred to the magazine. The title of the article in question turned out to be "A Vietnamese Lesbian Speaks." Phoning the NEA representative back, I asked, "Could the subject matter perhaps have something to do with it?" "Of course not!!!" She hung up and that was the end of the conversation. And that was the end of our funding from the NEA. Since the NYSCA grant and subscription money didn't cover costs, out came my credit card once again!

The next issue, titled *Anniversary Issue*, (*IKON* 10, 1989), focused on *Autobiography and Short Fiction*. Some of the writers represented were Janine Pommy Vega, Rosario Caicedo, Diane

Glancy, Safiya Henderson Holmes, and Carol Tarlen. Artwork was supplied by Valerie Maynard and Clarissa Sligh, and Amy Zuckerman contributed photo documentation, "Loiyangalani: Place of Contrast, "Place of Trees," about a small town/village resting on the southeastern shore of Lake Turkana, Kenya. In this issue, I included some work of my own, the first chapter of what would later become a memoir, *America's Child: A Woman's Journey through the Radical Sixties* (Curbstone, 2007).

Also included was Catherine De Maria's searing testimony in words and photos, "War Zone: Tompkins Square Summer '88." August 7, 1988, over 450 police charged peaceful protestors demonstrating against anti-gentrification and a midnight curfew on Tompkins Square Park, a curfew which had been designed specifically to displace the homeless sleeping there during a time of rampant homelessness in the area. The police rampaged through the neighboring streets, arresting passersby, the homeless, and residents. It was caught on video, but no policemen were ever convicted. It was the beginning of a month-long occupation of the surrounding neighborhood by the police. Catherine DeMaria's journal of those days remains an invaluable resource. One of her photos of that night is hauntingly reminiscent of Kent State—although fortunately, in this case, although many were badly hurt, no one was killed.

At this juncture, the *IKON* staff consisted of myself as editor, Rachel Guido deVries as the Fiction Editor, Kimiko Hahn as the poetry editor and continuing as contributing editors, Carole Byard, Beth Brant and Margaret Randall. We decided that since most of the readers of *IKON* might never have seen the first series of the magazine, *IKON* 11 (1990) *The Sixties: A Retrospective of IKON Series One 1966-1969* was an anthology of material selected from the seven Sixties issues. It opened with an essay by Margaret Randall, "Parallels from the Sixties to the Nineties," comparing the two series of *IKON*, which was only appropriate since she had been connected so closely with both, appearing in the first issues of both Series One and Two and as a contributing editor of Series Two. The introductory section of the issue also included an essay edited from an interview with Carole Byard, "On Being a Woman Artist of Color: The Sixties, The Seventies, Today."

We picked representative works from each of the seven issues, including political essays, poetry, articles, photo essays by Karl Bissinger, who was the *IKON* staff photographer at the time, a short story by Grace Paley, an essay by Diane Wakoski, "The Theater of Eternal Music: La Monte Young and Marian Zazeela," work from the Cuban Cultural Congress, Henry Flynt's Exercise Awareness-States—Flynt was the only man to appear in *IKON* Second Series 1, with his controversial essay, 'The Radicalism of Unbelief," and Haydée Santamaría's "Letter to Che," as well as "Letters from Minoko, about the anti-nuclear protests in Japan.

The logical next issue after the Sixties was the Nineties. The two issues were originally thought of as a piece with Carole Byard's piece in the Sixties issue as a transitional essay, recognizing that the *IKON* of the sixties, with all its "radicalism," did not represent either women or women of color adequately. Carole also was the co-ordinating editor of Coast to Coast. This was the last collaborative issue we did, and because of its length and scope (160 pages), *IKON* 12/13 (1991-1992) was published as a double issue. It was titled, *The Nineties: Moving Forward, Reaching Back/A Multicultural Odyssey*, with the subtitle, *Focus on Coast to Coast: National Women Artists of Color*. The issue's publication would run concurrently with Coast to Coast's exhibition, "Ancestors Known and Unknown: Box Works." Specific information about Coast to Coast exhibitions, along with the names of the over 200 women participating in the exhibitions, was listed at the back of the issue.

Besides artwork by twenty-three artists including Emma Amos, Tomie Arai, Josely Carvalho, Miriam Hernández, Yong Soon Min, Faith Ringgold, Beverly R. Singer, Clarissa Sligh, Diosa Summers, there were essays by Adrian Piper, "The Joy of Marginality," "The Hand of Memory in Some African American & Latina Art," by

Lucy R. Lippard, and "Seeing "Yellow": Asians and the American Mirror," by Margo Machida. Arlene Raven, bell hooks and Meena Alexander were also included.

Along with selections of fiction and poetry, there was a Latina Panel Carole Byard put together especially for *IKON*, which took place in Clarrisa Sligh's loft. Regina Araujo Corritore, Maria Elena Gonzalez, Miriam Hernandez, and Elaine Soto discussed their box works projects, leading into a more general discussion of themselves as Latina women artists. One of the artists, Regina Araujo Corritore, described how her box project "My Mother's Side" centered around her mother's history, a combination of Puerto Rican, Peruvian, and North American lineage. Using maps in the background, she chose to symbolize her mother in transition "as a bride."

Crossroads: An Anthology of Art for a Time of Transition & Change (*IKON* 14/15, 1993), a double issue, was our last. Among the contributors to the final issue were contributors from past issues, along with writers and artists who had not been published in *IKON* before. Both writers and artists from the New York community and nationwide were represented. Among the poets were Minrose Gwin, Pamela Sneed, Enid Dame, Kathy Engel, Anya Achtenberg and Anjail Ahmad, Meena Alexander, Steve Cannon, Jack Hirschman, Chris Brandt, Irena Klepfisz, Mary Jane Sullivan, Judith Clark, and Eileen Myles; essayists included Janice Gould and Margaret Randell. Altogether, twelve prose writers, forty-five poets, and eight artists were represented. After two series of the magazine, an anthology (*We Stand our Ground*), a series of chapbooks (Hettie Jones, Chuck Wachtel, Paul Pines, Martha King, Harry Lewis) and a series of poetry books (Rochelle Ratner, D.H. Melhem, Gale Jackson, Paul Pines, Kathy Engle, Bruce Weber), *IKON* was finally laid to rest, in part due to a bureaucratic tax form issue.

The usual tax procedure for *IKON*, which we had followed for more than twelve years, was just to send in a Charities Exemption Form since we didn't have enough revenue to have to fill out a

990. Because we hadn't filed the 990 for five years, a new requirement, though we never received the notice of change, we were notified we would have to go through the whole process of getting approval for tax-exempt status and file years back tax forms in order to continue. The only way to avoid the bureaucratic mess was to dissolve the corporation and close our bank account, so *IKON* officially became a part of history.

It is important to acknowledge the enormous amount of work that goes into any alternative press, many most often laboring without any monetary remuneration or little outside recognition, and the invisible hard work and incredible commitment of those who run alternate magazines and presses that keep the creative spirit alive. For those, like us at *IKON*, it meant the hours, the nights, (many times all night while, simultaneously working a daytime job) of work, without a paid staff or an office.

Looking at the complete run of the *IKON*, I am filled with pride—not personal pride, because a magazine is the work of not one, but many people, all those who contributed their artwork, their manuscripts, their love and labor because what *IKON* stood for was something they believed in. There were other wonderful magazines and presses at the time that honored the history and spirit of the creative women and activists of the period, that saw feminism as inexorably linked to issues of racism and classism: *Sinister Wisdom*, *Conditions*, Kitchen Table Press, Crossing Press, *Heresies* to mention only a few. I believe where *IKON* found its place in this plethora of creativity was in its dedication to the integrity of the picture and the word, separately and in combination, and its expansiveness, reaching ever beyond.

IKON, as its title implied, was a synthesis that brought together art and politics, creativity and change, pictures and words, and as a magazine, could reflect within months what was occurring in the cultural community, the local community and the world. For me, the second series, like the first, punctuated the end of an era. As the title *Crossroads* implied, it *was* a turning point. The cover, perfectly reflecting the synthesis that was *IKON*, was a beautiful sculpture by African American artist Carole Byard, who had created the artwork for the *Art Against Apartheid* issue and had played such an important part in the magazine, both editorially and artistically. Her cover graphically depicting unity in duality, the traveler and the proud warrior woman, refusing to be defeated.

A LOOK BACK AT *IKON*

Jan Clausen

When I look back over the issues of *IKON* Second Series, the word "freedom" comes to mind—and right after that, the word "maturity." There was such artistic and political maturity in both process and product! I think it's no accident that the Second Series launched in the early eighties. In all likelihood, such a project wasn't possible until Second Wave feminism got past the early stages of illuminating rage and wishful sisterhood--the naïve hope (admittedly almost exclusively a white phenomenon!) that simply acting in concert as women, as lesbians, would create a female utopia. In the pages of *IKON*, we see the idealistic yet realistic striving of feminist artists and organizers convinced that their love for each other and the world demands creative engagement with every kind of human being, every facet of power.

In saying this, I hope I'm not appearing to suggest that the journal came across as the vehicle of some abstract political program. I need to emphasize that its visual beauty and allure—and the purposeful juxtaposition of a wide range of forms, from photography to plays and from painting to poetry to fiction to performance—are absolutely outstanding. It's crucial to have the contents archived online, but nothing compares to the sensuous experience of holding the physical copies. Their high-quality paper was a delight for the hands as the page layouts were a delight for the eyes. Each issue of *IKON* is completely inviting, recommending itself to the senses long before the so-called content can be cognitively processed. There's a joy conveyed by the beauty at hand, even as the topics addressed, such as poverty, war, lesbian oppression, femicide, or apartheid, are often deadly serious.

In short, *IKON* did not merely showcase but actively (creatively) promoted further creativity.

Certainly, room was made for sophisticated analysis (as in Susan Sherman's introductory essay to the first issue of the second series, "Freeing the Balance: Activism and Art"), yet there was never a sense that this would be a venue for ideological wrangling. Instead, *IKON* espoused a non-dogmatic commitment to radical politics (a practice to uproot and replace the structures conditioning poverty, oppression, and the inability for individuals and peoples to determine their fates). The cultural politics of *IKON*: Second Series had significant commonalities with projects like *Conditions* magazine, Kitchen Table: Women of Color Press, and the anthology *This Bridge Called My Back: Writings by Radical Women of Color*, in terms of their expansive approach to women's experience, lesbian existence, and feminist leadership. Simply put, all of these projects affirmed that women's freedom is impossible to define or realize apart from humanity's freedom while rejecting the many patriarchal aspects of prior liberation movements. In this context, an embrace of theory and organizing on the basis of racial identity (like that sponsored by Kitchen Table Press, *This Bridge*, or *IKON* 9, the "Without Ceremony" issue guest edited by Asian Women United) was quite distinct from today's understanding of what might be labeled identitarian politics (i.e. a separatism based on essentialist definitions). While constituting a key resource for personal and collective growth, this type of organizing typically complemented ongoing coalition work, such as that modeled at an outstanding level in *IKON* 5/6, the special double issue on Art Against Apartheid.

As typified by that issue, *IKON*'s commitment to internationalism was unusual and inspiring. Susan's positive experience with the Cuban Revolution in the late 1960s no doubt influenced this orientation, but so did the lingering impact of the anti-Vietnam War movement, central to many of the artists showcased in *IKON*'s first series. Susan's decision to take on primary responsibility for sustaining the second series while working in dialogue with a rich creative community and at times sharing or entirely giving over editorial control probably allowed publication to continue as long as it did. At the same time, it involved a heroic outpouring of volunteer energy, such that the effort couldn't be indefinitely sustained.

IKON was a gathering in, a placing in conversation, of radical women's poems, stories, interviews, plays, photographs, drawings, paintings, and essays. It said: all of this is happening, all of this is possible, this is how women are bringing new worlds into being, together and across lines of difference, or in that solitude that summons future community. It was a window on the widest possibilities: the belief that all forms of power and modes of social organization, including those shaped by colonial histories within the U.S. and between North and Global South, are the business and responsibility of those traditionally shut out. Looking back, it's certainly striking to see how many legendary feminist artists were showcased here, but what strikes me more than the fame or prominence of individual contributions is how the pieces land in relation. It's not just: oh, Audre Lorde published "Poetry Is Not a Luxury" in *IKON*, but: here's what her essay was in dialogue with. Here's the creative context her insights came out of—without which, no matter her brilliance, they wouldn't have surfaced in the form that they did.

IKON made space for art and documentation from the Nicaraguan revolution, for Michelle Cliff's classic essay on Jamaican identity: "If I Could Write This in Fire, I Would Write This in Fire," for translated work by Catalán writer Mercè Rodoreda, and above all, for the incredibly moving artistic acts of solidarity with the South African freedom movement in issue 5/6. There is a sense of profound struggle threading throughout this work—if by that seemingly over-used noun is meant the concrete, often fumbling labor of constructing ways of life that actually function in the interests of life: good life not just for a few but for everyone. In other words, there's a bracing lack of romanticism in pieces that speak to the tough material realities of that effort, such as Carole Byard's interview reflecting on her formation as a Black woman artist or the

"Mothers' Roundtable" (from *IKON* 9, "Without Ceremony") featuring a discussion by New York-based Asian American women who
were raising children while working outside the home. Without
needing to invoke standard Left rhetoric, the magazine's perspective repeatedly aligned with the experiences, needs, and strengths
of poor and working-class subjects. The work is multi-textural and
invites an immersive focus that was rare back then and is much
rarer now in an age of wall-to-wall distractions.

The subtitle of the Art Against Apartheid issue is "Works for
Freedom," but it could have been the slogan for every other issue as well. What would freedom mean for women, for lesbians,
for artists, in all the specificity of their divergent circumstances, in
their connections to the full range of family, community, society,
and world? What would freedom look like, what would it sound
like, what would it cry out against? What histories would it draw
on? With whom would it stand in solidarity (among those currently living, but also the yet-to-be-born)? Here, I can see the importance of Susan's editorial affirmation of what was positive about
the "male-dominated" 1960s political and cultural left. *IKON* 11, the
retrospective Sixties issue, shows how radical artists of that era,
by blasting through the stultifying wall that Cold War politics had
built between creative expression and the exercise of power, did
an important bit of groundwork for lesbian and feminist cultural
insurgency.

I certainly don't want to idealize the eighties, the era of Ronald
Reagan, but I'm moved—and yes, nostalgic—at *IKON*'s record of a
pulse of creativity infused with the conviction: It must change! We
won't be prevented from remaking the world. We women must do
it ourselves; we must do it together. Despite what appear to be
limited means, our strength is in each other. *IKON* Second Series
was and is fearless, beautiful, generative—and more relevant than
ever in these dangerous and excessively captured times. (For, no
bones about it, we North Americans are now more firmly than ever
in the clutches of capitalist patriarchy, assaulted not only by right-

wing revanchism but by the liberal lies of a foundering U.S. empire that paints its bombers in rainbow colors.) Of course, it's never the case that the strategies of the past can be precisely replicated. Yet it means so much to have these elegant and tangible reminders of that which was and remains to inform the difficult work to come.

A LOVE POEM FOR SUSAN AND *IKON*

Gale Jackson

"We can and must create a new world with new forms, tech-niques, and ideas"
> —IKON Cover, Second Series, Volume1

... I got my head out the window and I'm hollering cause I know you're there to meet me downstairs and move on the world city borough prospect park west ... as the sun takes it down ...
> —from "housework," IKON, Second Series, Volume 2

"Hiya Gale. It's your old friend Susan."
Our routine greeting. We haven't "seen" each other for years now—the pandemic, life, coming into seniority in the city—but the connection is abiding, our friendship ever blossoming, the conversation, our shared house work and world creating, continuing.

A brilliant run of *IKON* magazine lives on a base shelf in my home book collection. When Susan calls, I return to them. Reveling in over forty years of conversation, imagination, voice and vision, connection, community, kinship, and communion.

A polyphonically global anti-racist full spectrum gender, sexuality, and ability affirming, womanist/feminist/humanist imagining, voice, and vision. A root and still singing poetics/visual art/aesthetics/politics of radical compassion. A singing towards social and environmental right relations, peace, justice, indigeneity and futurity. A telling of our stories over and trans-versing genre and medium, new and old forms, discipline and location. A radiantly generative gathering of women weaving worlds in conversation with and within a vibrant constellation of wonderfully multiply identified kin.

A singing.

Never thought about it at the time, but looking back at these volumes, I also see, hear, recognize, what has been, for me, a foundational gathering of beloved mentors, teachers, influence, inspiration, and lifelong companionship in songs, in voices, in visions, that have shaped my own: Audre Lorde singing, "Poetry is not a Luxury, Paula Gunn Allen singing, of "The Woman Who Owned the Shadows," June Jordan singing, of "The Cedar Trees of Lebanon," Alexis DeVeaux singing, of "Altars of Liberation," Karl Bissinger singing, Carole Byard, Valerie Maynard, Blanche Weisen Cook, bell hooks, Jewelle Gomez, Safiya Henderson-Holmes singing, Meena Alexander singing, Sekou Sundiata singing, Andrée Mclaughlin singing, of Medgar Evers, Black feminist activism, and the necessity of coalition. Susan singing of love and life and women and tech and design and form as meaning and art as action.

When Susan calls, I return to those volumes, this full voiced chorus of imagining and calling the world into being, and I again lose and find myself in the incantation, the poems and the fiction, and the essays, and the narrative weaving of storytelling in word and image, sound and visual inscription, in the calls and responding of hundreds of artists/thinkers/activists, all nested in *IKON* and Susan's visionary designing.

Looking back and looking forward, I am humbled and honored (and feeling very lucky!) to see hear know my own voice threaded throughout this weaving...and to see hear know, with immense gratitude, my own coming of age as an artist in that threading.

So, days later, I call Susan back.

"What was the question again?"

She laughs.

Who? What? How? Why?

A little about our storytelling...

Susan and me and *IKON*. A long-time friendship and a site of collaboration honed over four decades of conversation. And continuing. A beloved "old" friend, *companera*, and collaborator.

A journal which has been a critical site for the singing of a "new world" into being in a chorus of essential storytelling and conversations, and within that chorus, that singing, storytelling, that conversation, a critical site for the cultivation of my own public voice as a writer, a poet, a storyteller, a historian in a griot tradition.

We met (was it at an international solidarity cultural event at PS 41 in the West Village?) at a crossroads of women artists/activists in the early 80s in New York City, in a time of historic turning, social/economic/political contestation, nuclear danger, and environmental reckoning, anti-colonial struggle, artistic/intellectual/political explosion, community organizing and empowerment, cultural activism, international solidarity, protest and demonstration, uprising and liberation. Susan was embarking on the second series of the *IKON* publication, and I was a co-coordinator of an international cultural education project in support of South African liberation called Art Against Apartheid. Our connection was organic (maybe Susan asked me for work maybe I heard her reading her poems/saw *IKON*, and submitted a poem called "housework"), and we have been talking, dancing, singing, together ever since.

We locked arms, hearts, and minds.

Susan/*IKON* became deeply engaged collaborators in the work of Art Against Apartheid (organizing some extraordinary community-based readings!), and together, with Scott Barton, Blaise Tobia, and the design work of George "Geo" Smith, we co-edited a special issue/anthology called Art Against Apartheid: Works for Freedom bringing the voices of an international chorus of voices in support of South African liberation into conversation with the voices and works of South African artists. That was in 1986 following (and very much a part of) two years of cultural organizing and events in which over 11,000 artists and community organizations participated.

Over the years, we seeded and cultivated a number of what remain my most treasured conversations, relationships, and artistic projects in collaboration with Susan and *IKON*, including my ongoing work in narrative historical poems on the lives of African American women: beginning with "a song for Phillis Wheatley."

In 1988, Susan/*IKON* invited Kimiko Hahn and me to collaborate on a conversational collection that led to the publication of our anthology volume *We Stand Our Ground: Three Women, Their Vision, Their Poems.* Susan invited Josely Carvalho to illuminate the text with her artwork. And our collaborative conversations continued as we mourned and organized through that first pandemic of our youth, as we carried the names and songs of our peers who became ancestors too soon throughout decades of singing in publication. In the 90s, Susan/*IKON* collaborated with Carole Byard, Clarissa Sligh, and "Coast to Coast: National Women Artists of Color," another beautiful volume, and with Susan/*IKON*'s invitation (in 2003), we published a volume of my poems, called *Suite for Mozambique*, which contains a substantial number of reproductions of Carole Byards's "Rent" series paintings... This would be one of our last collaborations with Carole on what the Abenaki call this earth walk...

Still, our voices live and sing together in these volumes. And, over the years, in the occasional celebratory reading. And now in our archiving. A gathering of old friends. Still imagining a new world into being.

Yes, dear Susan, let's please keep talking. With love...

IKON: A PASSAGEWAY

Demetria Martinez

I was a shy, budding poet in my early twenties, searching through the shelves of bookstores for the meaning of life. And sure enough, I was finding it, specifically in the poetry section at the women's bookstore in Albuquerque called Full Circle: Janice Gould, Gloria Anzaldúa, Audre Lorde, Paula Gunn Allen, Sonia Sanchez and more. If I couldn't afford to buy a book of poetry, I perused it, as all visitors were welcome to do. Thus began my education in women's studies, an education not only of the head but of the heart. That is to say, my learning thrust me into a world in which women loving women was not only acceptable but celebrated.

So, one can imagine my excitement when I saw a flyer announcing a reading at the store by Susan Sherman, poet and editor of the radical women's magazine *IKON*. While waiting for the reading to start, I looked at some samples of the magazine. To my delight, I saw the names of feminist poets I had come to admire during my hours at Full Circle published in *IKON*. I took a seat on the floor of the crowded bookstore.

What came forth as Susan read was a vision that was at once contemplative and revolutionary: a call to reflect and a call to act, to act on behalf of change. Her poems extolled a politics rooted in passion, a passion rooted in female desire. This stunning energy came through in all her work. Typical was the poem "What I Want," that I would read and reread as I became increasingly familiar with Susan's work over time. I was struck by lines expressing a gentle yet powerful plea:

Please for a moment relieve me of
constant discovery   this prison
perception   But I am grounded in myself

this world I was born to   my passion
for change   to change things
the need to touch   hold   be touched
held.

I was amazed at how she could start out with what seemed like a simple love poem, only to have it open out into a statement about identity. I had not yet come to realize my own identity as a lesbian. I was originally drawn to *IKON* by its diverse and internationalist content. I believe that somehow, at a subconscious level, a door was being opened by lesbians' work I would come to know, represented in *IKON* not only by poets and artists, but by numerous articles and essays like Huong Giang Nguyen's, "A Vietnamese Lesbian Speaks" in *IKON* 9 *Without Ceremony* published in collaboration with Asian Women United, the many beautiful love poems of Audre Lorde, Adrienne Rich, Rachel Guido deVries, Margaret Randall and so many others, as well as Susan's own essay, "Women, Culture, Identity: A Re-examination," in double issue 12/13, *The Nineties: Moving Forward, Reaching Back.*

At the time, I was a religion reporter covering the faith-based Sanctuary Movement; in the course of my research I had accompanied a Lutheran minister to the U.S.-Mexico border where he helped two refugees enter the U.S. The women were fleeing right-wing death squads funded by the U.S. in the name of fighting "communism." I was indicted and was facing 25 years in prison. Finally, after a two-week trial, I was acquitted on First Amendment grounds: freedom of the press. I would later publish my first novel, *Mother Tongue*, based loosely on my experiences with the Sanctuary Movement. Other books came later, including collections of poetry, essays, and short stories.

So I found that, as well as speaking to my lesbian identity, what drew me to *IKON* was finding my Latina/Chicana identity so richly represented in articles, essays and poems. For example, the amazing *IKON* 12/13 focusing on Coast to Coast, the National Women of

Artists of Color, in particular the panel of Latina artists discussing the boxes they had contributed to the "Ancestors' Known and Unknown: Box Works."

That fateful reading at Full Circle was not the last time I would hear Susan present her work. We met up again in Willimantic, Connecticut, where she participated in a poetry reading sponsored by the leftist Curbstone Press. I was on the board of the press at that time. We would later publish Susan's memoir, *America's Child: A Woman's Journey Through the Radical Sixties,* a book that joined the ranks of Curbstone's work by poets and writers from around the world. Again, as in the reading at Full Circle, Susan's work centered female desire.

In 2016, Susan and I were invited to participate in the American Educational Studies Association (AESA) Conference in Seattle, Washington by SEW (The Society for Educating Women-- an international and inter-generational community of learning and inquiry), who sponsored a special session, "Feminist Publishing Under the Gun: A Retrospective Conversation Over *IKON's* Legacy Educating Women."

In spring 2016, SEW published a special issue of original and reprinted poems, essays, and short stories by *IKON* contributors and others who share *IKON's* commitment to social change. I co-edited that issue with Susan, giving me the opportunity to add Jessica Helen Lopez, Mary Oishi, Andrea Serrano, Andrea L. Mays and Daisy Zamora as new contributors. I came to understand and appreciate the work that goes into curating a magazine and physically shaping it.

Before *IKON*, I had been mostly familiar with leftist publications featuring writers from Latin America. Afterwards, I discovered *Sinister Wisdom, Conditions, 13th Moon, Trivia, off our backs,* and a whole host of other publications, each uniquely fitting together in the mosaic that was women's publishing at the time. *IKON* opened the world of women's publishing to me.

MEMORIES OF WHO AND WHERE WE WERE

Margaret Randall

If you look up *icon* or *Ikon* in the dictionary, you will find it defined as, "a representative symbol . . . worthy of veneration." Design considerations led the creators of *IKON Magazine* to spell the word with a *k*. In speaking of their motivation, the editors said: "For us the word *IKON* symbolized synthesis—words and pictures, art and politics, creativity and change, the separate parts fused as one into a unity in which all the parts could be perceived simultaneously, the way you perceive a picture. We believed there was no conflict between theory and art, art and action." They wanted to remove the middleman and thought that artists were perfectly capable of understanding and writing about their own work.

It's important to accurately historicize the latter claim. Today, we have a proliferation of brilliant critics and a body of analysis that is key to understanding who we are and what we do. Many of them are from our own generation. I am thinking of Susan Sherman herself, Audre Lorde, Mark Behr, Lucy Lippard, and Roberto Tejada, among others. In the 1960s, the criticism to which we had access was almost exclusively written by dilettante or highly biased "experts," many of whom defended interests opposed to ours. Today, important critiques such as critical race theory are among the topics feared by neofascistic forces, illustrating how thinking itself is manipulated by the politics of the moment.

IKON Magazine, in both its 1965 -1969 and 1982 -1994 iterations, was a periodic print venue for what mattered at a time that has been referred to as the age of the critic, not the artist, of analysis, not originality. It was a time in which the mainstream had moved fast toward a mind-dulling coercive message aimed at separating us from our most genuine values and creative powers.

IKON Magazine represented the absolute best of who, where, and how we were in a decade of turmoil and change. The work it published was often ground-breaking, always excellent. It's an extraordinary experience to enter the Lesbian Poetry Archive today and rediscover its power, especially as we are living in another endangered era, one that particularly targets the rights of women and other marginalized groups. Following the restrictive, often stultifying 1950s, embodied by McCarthyism's destructive scourge, the 1960s exploded in resistance and liberating visions. These were developed more fully in the decades to come.

It's not surprising that this entire period produced many literary journals, poets, visual artists, singer/songwriters, theater groups and other creative efforts. We were concerned with our social ills and explored our responses in our work. Biased historians have too often distorted the 1960s, portraying it as a decade of irresponsible drug-induced bedlam, predictably downplaying or deleting its more political nature. Distortion of the sixties necessarily led to distortions of the seventies, eighties, and nineties. When we go back to the source—and *IKON* is an important part of that source—we can clearly see what was at stake and are able to read many of the powerful voices that were present.

Each discreet cultural project of the 1960s, consisting of leftists, artists, poets, pacifists, those fighting racial injustice, back-to-the-earthers, folks experimenting with mind-expanding drugs, lesbian feminists, and others, used their avenues of expression to advertise particular ideologies or interests. Often, these projects were composed of small cliques mostly interested in promoting their own work. In both its series, *IKON* actively sought new talent and published some of the most exciting work of the times.

One noteworthy aspect of both *IKON* runs was how they crossed lines. The second series reflected a wide-ranging multicultural cross border lesbian feminist sensibility that was also multigenre, multi-generational, sensitive to a variety of struggles, and stunningly put together. *IKON* didn't just talk about "the other" it published work by Native American, African American, Asian American, and Hispanic writers and artists, and paid tribute to cultural and political struggles being waged beyond our borders. It featured Queer work before that term was even used. It explored the different feminisms in these communities. It always included enough work by each contributor so readers would have a real sense of what that person was about. This wide-ranging vision also created a broad network that early on began making the connections that turned out to be so valuable over time.

I know something about the challenges of producing this sort of publication back then. When *IKON's* first series was flourishing in New York City, my own literary quarterly, *El Corno Emplumado / The Plumed Horn*, was going strong in Mexico City. Mexican poet Sergio Mondragón and I met at a nightly literary salon hosted by Surrealist poet Philip Lamantia. Poets of different latitudes read to one another, but few of us knew the others' language well enough to understand the subtleties. We immediately saw the need for a magazine that would feature good translation. *El Corno* was born.

Susan visited us in 1967, and she and I forged an enduring relationship at the Cultural Congress of Havana in 1968. A half-century later, we continue to be in close touch, and I continue to benefit not only from our friendship but from Susan's brilliant mind.

From our initial contact, *IKON* and *El Corno* nurtured and supported one another. In the pages of *IKON*, we stayed in touch with what was happening north of the border. In *El Corno*, *IKON's* readers kept abreast of what was going on in the global south. By the time *IKON's* second series came along, I was in Cuba and later back in the US. I was able to be closer to the magazine and, for a while, served on its advisory board.

Just as for *IKON*, it was important for *El Corno* to cross borders (many of them created by neocolonialism), draw from a variety of literary tendencies and voices, and create a network that linked creative peoples worldwide. One of the ways in which the establishment tried to control the publication of magazines—pages where people were able to try out ideas, present choices different from those being pushed by officialdom, present their art, and create forums for discussion—was by having their own institutions own and fund them.

Producing a truly independent publication was extremely difficult. It entailed a continuous search for financial support. Susan started *IKON* second series with a small inheritance and wound up having to declare personal bankruptcy after it ended; such was her passion for the project. *IKON* and *El Corno*, along with all the other outlier independents, always had to struggle for grants, stipends from institutions that wouldn't interfere with what we wanted to publish, subscriptions from readers and libraries, and, in our case, advertisements from friends. Running such a publication meant not only seeking new work, editing, and designing; it also involved raising money, keeping up with correspondence, overseeing the printing, handling distribution, and every other part of the project.

It's also worth noting that this was long before the internet, email, and modern printing methods existed. We used letterpress and linotype. We depended on the postal services of the era, and I remember from my experience with *El Corno* that it took three to four months for an envelope of poems to reach us from Buenos Aires or New York and the same amount of time for our acceptance or rejection to reach the poet who had submitted them. Everything was slower, more laborious, and difficult. Yet *IKON* was full of exciting innovation. It was always elegantly designed and beautifully produced.

Those of us with successful independent projects were also forced to contend with serious right-wing pushback. *El Corno* lost 500 subscriptions promised by the Pan American Union (cultural arm of the Organization of American States). They demanded that we not publish work from Cuba, and when we refused, they cut us off. *El Corno* had to stop publishing after we supported Mexico's 1968 student movement. The following year, I barely escaped Mexico with my life, had to go underground and eventually sought refuge in revolutionary Cuba.

In New York, *IKON*'s storefront office was vulnerable to a similar attack. During the first series, Susan endured FBI informants who told lies about her involvement with several struggles of the day. Many years later, when the Freedom of Information Act made it possible for her to access her FBI files, one could scoff at some of the more absurd accusations they contained. At the time, those accusations meant the demise of *IKON*'s first series; Susan lost her job and became seriously ill. Many of our projects were forced to shut down, and unfortunately, the first series of *IKON* has not been digitized, making the Lesbian Poetry Archive all the more valuable in allowing us to understand work that continues the tradition of the first, presenting work that was unique and, in many cases, prophetic.

Although she started the magazine with Nancy Colin (who left after the first series) and had other collaborators from time to time, Susan Sherman was *IKON*'s mother, and the magazine's second series was a bright star in feminist publishing. Susan's editing and design skills made the magazine a gem of quality and beauty. One opened each breathtaking issue and found poetry, prose, photographs and other visual arts, musical scores, interviews, letters and more. They seduced the reader with innovatively designed pages.

The connections were important. So much of our evolving consciousness and so many of our important struggles were present in the work of *IKON* contributors such as Adrienne Rich, Audre Lorde, Judith Malina, Hettie Jones, Jewelle Gomez, Cherríe Moraga, Claudia Gordillo, Fay Chiang, June Jordan, among others. Today, the archive remains a compendium of voices—many gone, others still with us—of the great talents of an era. And as such, it speaks to us of what may be possible now, in this new time of turmoil, resistance, and change.

I feel fortunate and proud to have published in *IKON* several times. A half-century later, I review our collaborations and am impressed with how well they hold up. Often, when we reread what we and others wrote so long ago, we are embarrassed; the sentiments may continue to feel authentic, but the way we expressed them outmoded or cliched. Not so with *IKON*. I am astonished at how contemporary these collaborations seem. A strong present is always built upon a strong past. This is true for poetry and art as in any other field. Reading *IKON* today is as energizing and rewarding as it was five decades ago.

A POEM THAT STARTS IN WINTER

Susan Sherman

This is a poem for people without a history
Whatever their color   Whatever their race
Who can't remember their mother ever holding them
Talking to them about their past
Who find themselves in unknown places
Without instructions & without a guide

This is a poem for the children of immigrants
Whose parents wanted so much to forget   to leave behind
The places they were born   the places they fled
They never spoke of those days to their children
Never even told them their grandparents' names
Who died leaving their children lost   and restless
Rootless   hungry

This is a poem that starts in winter
But never ends   A poem about people
About individuals   With specific features
Proper names

This is a poem for Sarah whose mother was Jewish
but no one could tell
She had blond hair blue eyes   It was 1939
She taught Sarah a lesson about vision
How to make people see past you   How to hide
In moments of doubt they would always throw it in your face
You could count on it
"Dirty Jew"

This is a poem about words

This is a poem about Sarah's mother
Who never stepped inside a synagogue after the age of eight
Who never forgave her own parents for what she was born
An immigrant   poor
Who lived her contradictions until the day she died
Who left her lie behind her   A legacy drawn
In her daughter's face

This is a poem for Sarah's mother   A poem about words

This is a poem for Barbara   1961   Whose father warned her
If she was involved with those radicals at Berkeley   those "Reds
He would be the first to give her name to the FBI   To turn her in
She never doubted he was serious   She learned that day never to trust
& never to speak

This is a poem about trust

This is a poem for Carole who cried out in shame
Discovering her ancestors had killed & robbed
To gain a country   Carole who had a history
She no longer wished to claim

This is a poem for a Vietnamese poet   Havana, 1969
Who praised three young Americans for their courage
Standing against their own country   their own people
For what they felt right
He had no choice   was forced to fight   No virtue in that
They thought him too generous   mistaken at best   But still it helped
But still it healed

It was winter then too

This is a poem about digging images from rage   when all else fails
When there is no common past

An anger imbedded so deeply
It survives

This is a poem about war

This is a poem for Brenda who fell in love with a woman
Years before it became a political act
Who decades later still stumbles over words long forbidden
Jealous of those who proclaim their love nonchalantly
"Lesbian"

This is a poem for Brenda
This is a poem about words
A poem about winter   A poem about war

This is a poem for those caught between worlds
Squeezed between times   For people without a history
Who connect with no ancestral past

This is a poem about them   about me

This is a poem about words like dialogue compassion
which have yet to appear   but people this poem
About war contradiction rage choice anger
Trust

This is a poem that starts in winter
But never ends

This is a poem about people individuals
with specific features
Proper names

BORDER GUARDS

Susan Sherman

There are lines drawn in the sand
that must never be crossed   So say the pundits
the arbiters of boundaries definitions   of what should
or should not be said   or done   There are lines
drawn on maps   around cities boroughs neighborhoods
blocks houses   The people who live in them

There are lines drawn around nations
Lines teeming with people waiting to get in
or out   There are lines drawn around individuals
ethnic racial tribal lines   Around genders   he she they
you me them   A demarcation of countries
cultures continents

There are lines drawn around hemispheres
North South East West   Around the Earth itself
There are longitude lines   latitude lines
The Tropic of Capricorn is a line   The Tropic of Cancer
The earth as it circles space   As we delineate the seasons

A child takes a crayon   weighs it carefully in her palms
It is yellow the color of the sun   or of her dreams
places she sees in the pictures she thumbs through at night
her fingers scrolling color across paper   purple
then blue   an ocean   then fire blazing orange
subtle green trees   flowers   objects without set form
Only she knows what they mean

Lines of memory are like that   vivid weightless
ghost images without boundary Cezanne

seeing a forest of trees come into being
in the dawning sun   paints them obsessively
branches leaves undulating out of birthing light
as they come alive in front of his discerning eyes

All this is not to say we do not need to name things
identify them ourselves   but where exactly are these
boundaries borders   guarded so carefully
with passports rules and laws These lines that
label us define us   separate us These lines
that must never be crossed

FIRST AND LAST POEMS

Susan Sherman

for *Violeta Parra*

there is nothing romantic
about death about pain
tears falling like soft clouds
like copper clouds the color of rusted blood
the texture of fire

the first enemy is fear
the second power
the third old age

all my life   all those books all those feelings
words thoughts experiences
to say such simple words to feel
such simple things

your mountains like my own like home
rows of dust of light brown soil
as if a gentle wind could level them
could blow them away

the sea   touching my nostrils
filling them a country of smell
of sound of wine   flowers of salt air
of early morning opening and
opening through my mind
my heart the extremities
of my hands my feet

if I were a bird and could float
dipping and weaving tapestries of air
and light   if we could fly together
like silver crows birds of dream
until everything stops is silent and
gentle   like your songs your voice

but the world allows us nothing
the world is nerves   is fiber
dust and sand the world changes constantly
nothing remains the same

I see you singing into the air
as if your voice could fly   be free
were there creatures above you
listening fishing your gifts
from the breeze   was there a place
that could hold you as you opened yourself
to it   as you went where no one else
could follow   where no one else
could see

> *each time I have loved*
> *I have left part of myself behind*
> *until now I am mostly memory*
> *mostly dream   what I have left*
> *I give to you   my last love*
> *my last song*
>
> *the total of all*
> *I have ever felt or known*

we grow smaller as we grow

as things empty themselves of us
and we   of them

it is so deep   this thing between us
no name can contain it
even time trembles
at its touch

PHOTOGRAPHS BY DAKOTA SEBOURN

A Curious Devil

A Summoning Through the Gate

Pain Sequestration

NEW LESBIAN WRITING

SPIRIT IN THE DARK:
ARETHA FRANKLIN AS SPIRIT GUIDE

Shariananda Adamz

Aretha Franklin's 1970 recording of the foot-stomping pop gospel, "Spirit in the Dark" opens with a sultry inquiry: "Are you getting the spirit, the Spirit in the dark?" On the surface, the song is about following the impulse to dance, letting the unseen force of this music take your feet, hands, and body from entranced stasis to unguarded stimulation. "Spirit in the Dark" showcases an undulating jazz bass, piano accompaniment, spell-binding tambourine, a relentless cymbal, and rapacious drums. Aretha's growling riffs, scaling dives, and exalted high notes rise and fall so as to tap into the energy centers of any listener.

Aretha starts with a slow litany and asks "Are you getting the spirit?" "Are you getting it in the dark?" ("...*Moving, grooving, getting it in the dark?"*). It is clear that Aretha is speaking to those who "do it". That is "get down" and dirty; do the wild thing. In these lyrics we sense the intimation of sexual interactions driven by hungry lust, pressured by forces that are hardly holy. In these lines Aretha intimates that sometimes "getting the spirit in the dark" is to do the hidden, to cloak your actions under the cover of night. Aretha suggests that experiencing the spirit in the dark can be lonely, but also sensual and expansive - like looking up at a full moon sky haunted by smoky clouds.

In "Spirit in the Dark" Aretha seems to be talking about *the idea of spirit*; she may mean God or the Holy Spirit. Then again, she may mean "spirit" as in a *collective belonging. That is, the zest of true believers or the shared, buddy-girl team spirit. But* I think a truer definition as to what Aretha means is "spirit" as an impulse. Her music carries the spirit, often referred to as "soul." There are many souls walking the planet to the beat of Aretha's music. The consensus among us is that she was the "Queen of Soul. "Aretha embodied the word "soul" and her presence did more than entertain us. It guided us as would a great candle. Aretha was our "Spirit in the Dark."

In this song, she is not only talking about soul (hers, mine, yours, ours). She is talking to the inner self. Here, "moving with the spirit" is advice. If we are reminded of our spiritual training, especially by this "Spirit in the Dark," then we are on the right frequency and path. Aretha uses multiple meanings to reach those listening for inspiration, motivation, and to find joy. Yet above all else, this song's broad appeal appears to advocate freedom. With the lyrics "Tell me, sister, how do ya feel? Tell me my brother... How do you feel?" she is drawing us into a circle. Whenever she is stricken by a sanctified holler, we find resonance within ourselves, within Aretha, with Heaven, and anyone who shares our joining in the world. Whatever oppressions we have suffered--racial or societal, psychological or internal – we know she has too. She was a representative spirit, an ambassador of soul. As they called Gandhi a great soul, so we call Aretha, the Queen of Soul.

I speak here and now about Aretha's work because it nudges me. She has been gone only a short time but I miss her, and I cannot play her music enough to fill the chasm. I dream of her and I feel her spirit speaking to me. She has been the essential, unmistakable sound track of my life. It is her songs that I sing when I wash dishes, or shower, or make beds, or walk my doggie. It is her songs that I play and replay on my phone or record player. Finding myself as a lesbian and grappling with my heterosexual identity made me listen to Aretha as a truth teller.

Every time I hear "Spirit in the Dark," I surrender to it. I slip back into my church roots, into closed-eyed visions of raucous gospel choirs and some blessed three-tier- soprano. I see how the pianist and singer righteously amplify the sermon, and the Voice of God is present like an immense hallelujah heartbeat. I savor those holy times when my eyes and heart were open, when my fingers snapped, my foot patted, feeling involuntarily the God within.

But, as I have said, my reaction to "Spirit in the Dark" is also sexual. In the unfathomable mix of virtuous emotion and undeniable arousal lies the ineffable force of God where all things are one. I feel like bumping and grinding and doing the holy dance, like prancing on one foot and hopping about with the other. I feel like I am being pulled by my hair upwards into the cosmos; yet, at the same time, my belly and my vulva are being drawn down to the earth. This is akin to ascension or soul travel. When Aretha sings "Rise Sally rise ..Put your hands on your hips, cover your eyes" I get up and get ready to dance. I pantomime the lyrics. Of all of Aretha's songs, this is one of my favorites to dance to, sing along with, allow myself to be possessed by. In this way, Aretha has become a spirit guide within me.

When I hear Aretha sing "Spirit in the Dark," I revisit the smoky night clubs of my youth, slow dragging with the one I loved, snuggled up too closely, throbbing for what I dare not allow to happen. You, Aretha, have taught me lust, restraint, pause, and pardon. You have contributed to my wisdom. You have taught me about being "a natural woman," in my case, a woman-loving woman. Ah, those days, that feeling. This is how you have come to advise me in recent times.

Spirit in the Dark: Myself as a Dimensional Being

In the l960s, I listened to the radio a great deal. There was not much to do in the rural South except do as one's elders told one, attend church, and learn housekeeping. In offtimes I would cuddle up with a book and my transistor radio. One afternoon, as I cruised through the living room, the radio in arm, your first and newly released 45 rpm record was announced by the DJ. "And now "It Won't Be Long"" (Columbia, l961) a new release by Miss Aretha Franklin."

"Baby, here I am, by the railroad track! Waiting for my baby. He's coming back." The piano percussion like giant feet stomped into the room. That R&B fused with the gospel piano syncopation immediately took me to heaven. I vibrated like a plucked string on a bass fiddle, and there born was my unalterable connection with you.

Not until my late fifties did I come to relate music to spiritual frequencies. I am told celestial bodies have an interstellar symphony that can be heard as the music of the spheres. Some archaeologists believe the ancient megalithic stones of the Pyramids, Stonehenge, and Easter Island were set in place by tonal configurations of sound.

In my travels seeking the truth of God through various faiths and denominations, I discovered Buddhist chanting, the music of the spheres, the correlation between the chakra system and the scales of notes assigned to them. I learned that any sound has a vibration which can be harnessed to heal, to direct energy, to destroy. I learned that my very cells work to a mathematical equation that can be calibrated to music. I learned that sound and light are twin aspects of the Godhead.

But my journey was never without you, Aretha. Your music followed me everywhere. I carried you with me from college through graduate school, from postdoctoral studies to my further transformations. I consider you my first awakening. You have been with me like a guardian angel, singing songs that made up the principal soundtrack of my life: "You know I love you from A-Z" (So Swell When You're Well)" (Atlantic, Hey Now, Hey, l973). I collected your albums. Twice we met. Many times you have come to me in dreams.

I have lived long stretches of my life seeking myself and defining myself. I have made my own rules where needed and modified myself where other behavior was demanded. Along my path, like so many stepping stones, the trials were born and maturated in the testimony of your music.

I took the abusive theme in the lyrics of "I Never Loved a Man" to be "I never have been loved." Your hurt was my hurt. Your pain, my pain. I took "Running Out of Fools" to be an anthem of self-revelation and escape from self-delusion. You helped me accept myself, to realize that I did not deserve to be hurt, or to hurt myself with poor self-esteem, negative inner self talk that judged me and would not forgive me.

You have so soulfully written and selected songs that touch the nerve of human experience that I find compelled to make you know how deep the individual songs and the collected albums reach into the psyche of at least one soul. Your music has depicted the human condition at its worst ("I Never Loved a Man" Atlantic, 1967), and the hope and salvation in finding one's way, ("Sisters Are Doing it for Themselves", 1986). With "The Sister from Texas" (Atlantic, 1973) you empowered me as a survivor of incest, neglect, and a suicide attempt. I want you to know just how strong your music has made me.

I don't know about our past lives, Aretha. I don't know if any of us millions of fans know you from spiritual lives beforehand. It does not matter because you have made this one life real. I am no longer a spirit wandering in the dark. I am a soul, like you, going from relationship to relationship, from one educational and spiritual quest to another. I am gathering the stuff of my life as I prepare for homegoing (when I am called), but I don't want to leave without acknowledging how I have come out of many dark places and into the light on the gospel rhythms of your mighty voice .(I Say a Little Prayer for You", Atlantic,1974) That summer day in Alabama, when I first heard you sing, woke me to my own vibration, my propensity to feel and heal using the great music box of my soul.

For me, Aretha's voice is a predestined instrument of God. It led African-Americans through the turbulent 60s and through to the 21st Century. Aretha sang for the President of the United States, for Pope Francis, and performed at Carnegie Hall in New York. She seems to have a particular destiny, as much as did Rosa Parks . Her life is a testimony to an "Amazing Grace", but few would call her as I do, a Spirit Guide.

This phrase, part of the new thought terminology, means one advocates for good and fights the evils of hunger, poverty, bigotry, class, and racial difference. A spiritual guide fights wrongdoing in high places. They might be an angel, minister, or common folk, including the Lord Jesus Christ, Buddha, Lakshmi, and Parvati.

Many others have testified to Aretha's great divahood; so, I add my voice to the choir. It is, in part, how my Spirit has come to recognize its emergence from a long, dark tunnel of trial and tribulation, from traditional beliefs to a multi-denominational faith. All things work together for good, I am told.

Before she left this life, Aretha knew the exact breadth and depth of her own spirituality. Hers was a life baptized by tribulations, wholly washed in love and creativity, and sanctified by a serpentine fire that burned away the effects of soul-killing racial attacks and unkindness to women. She knew. She has helped me to know.

THE METAMORPHOSIS OF SCHRÖDINGER'S CAT

Cris Hernández

Schrödinger's cat was
            minding its own business
        hanging out inside the Box,
Not quite Alive, not quite Dead.

And then she discovered
                she had thoughts.

She thought about remembered things:
        the sight of the orange visage of a blood moon
        the feel of a hand smoothing her calico fur
        the sound in her body when she purred
        the warmth of the lazy autumn sun.

And she thought about the Box:
        dark as a closed, empty closet
        tight as the grip of a Victorian corset
        quiet as the space between the nighttime stars
        cold as a snowdrift in the spiraling wind.

She realized as she thought—
                    I am more than this box.
So Schrodinger's cat emerged
                quietly and discreetly.
        She broke free
and became.

GIVE ME THE MAN, FROM *MOROCCO*, 1930

Cris Hernández

Oh, Marlene!

The way you wore a tux
        changed everything for me.

The slow saunter coming out
        from behind the curtain

The way you gathered the room
        into the domain of your gaze

The audience churning at a woman
        daring to own the space

You take a puff from an unfiltered cigarette
        holding it like you own the air

And your gaze never waivers.

Taking your time, you stride to the tables
        where the men wear tuxedos

You start to sing "Give me the man. . ."
        gliding to sit in front of the ladies now

(Gary Cooper looks around, grinning to the guys—
        thinking she's singing about him)

You straddle the railing and take an offered drink
        consuming it in one tilt of the glass

A woman giggles while you survey her
                    a smoldering look in your eyes

You take the flower from behind her ear—
                    then ask if you may have it

Burying your face in the flower
                    you inhale the fecund scent

Her chin in your hand, she looks up at you
                    as you bend to kiss her lips

She giggles again, demurely hiding her gaze
                    at you from behind her fan

You flick your top hat and smile at her
                    your success lauded by the crowd.

I want to be like you, Marlene.
                    I want to wear that tux.

THE LETTERS

Kara Olson

—with references to May Sarton, Juliette Huxley, Emily Dick-inson, Susan Huntington, Virginia Woolf, Vita Sackville-West, Carson McCullers, Molly Malone Cook, Lorraine Hansberry, and Mary Oliver

I read and read until my hands ached
keeping the books open, until I was like May

and Juliette frozen in between separation and reunion:
our only reality to each other must be by letter.

Goodbyes were fraught and sacred: *boundlessly*
yours; my love tenderly; your devoted; with a kiss.

This was my inheritance. No sanctification.
Open me carefully Emily left in a note to Susan.

I read words from Virginia to Vita, from Vita
to Virginia and did not want them to stop.

I cried when I read that Annemarie was left out
of Carson's story. The photos Molly took of Lorraine.

Have you seen them? Lorraine is singing, is free
and playful in the presence of her beloved. Fear

was nowhere near, though two women in love
created an omen of violence.

Mary wrote about Lorraine changing Molly:
I believe she loved totally and was loved totally.

We see Mary's love for Molly in her poems. Years later,
Molly saw Lorraine on television and broke down.

Oh I did always think I would / see her again
and hear her voice again but, / Not in this world.

Were Lorraine and Molly like Virginia and Vita,
finding spiritual transformation in each other?

My kin wrote by candlelight and protected each other.
Women whose gazes were turned inward

or outward upon each other. Why did it take
so long to admit their love into our lives?

ON THE WAY TO SISSETON

Kara Olson

The dog, resting on the backseat,
blinks languidly, closes her eyes.
Alfalfa fields. Then soy. Corn

knee-high. Blond horses fighting flies.
You would love this hot day. This slow
intersection where nothing happens.

Later, my uncle will want his son-in-law,
his hired man, to clear a field on July 4th.
Even though my family doesn't hug,

or say I love you, we covet a day's work
alongside those closest to us. I imagine
you could write this story.

You were like that toward the end.
Have I told you? At night, I write
the words of my favorite novelists,

tending their thoughts like God does ours.
Like you did mine; how I read you.
Words count as much as the body.

Grace was how you took me.
My renewed encounter with wilderness.
When I arrive, my mother tells the story

of the antlered deer that swam
across the lake. All stealth in moonlight.
I don't dare talk about you, our love.

My hooves, too, I want to say, turned
into fins, transformed as I was like any
ordinary mammal by celestial things.

PORTRAIT OF YOUR AUNT MARGARET

Kit Kennedy

Bawdy as hell, head full of hail
and thunder. Known by the family
as *Your Aunt Margaret*. She spent
her life sending postcards from
strangely named towns of tiny pockets
and dim windows. Outposts where
the odd ones played starring roles.
She fit right in with her bizarre way
of speaking, bits of words twirling
in a kerfuffle. Hats with plumes
and feathers. Why she never
returned to her hometown,
mystery and blessing.

Every mirror in the house screams
I'm a spitting image of my namesake.
My closet with 5 pairs of identical
shoes says I walk in her footsteps.
In every third dream we meet
at a nondescript café in a train station,
silently sip tea, consider the one we face
strange.

WOMEN WHO LOVE PAPER

Kit Kennedy

for Carmencita Lozano

Women who love paper, love
to cook. Begin with suggested
ingredients: wood, cotton, flax,
straw, linen, jute, coarse grass,
even elephant poo. Make the pulp
combine with water, flatten, dry,
cut into sheets. As every woman
knows all things from kitchen
to bedroom improve with a healthy
dollop of imagination.

Here's where the fun starts: scribble,
draw, fold, cut, tear, scrunch, paste.
You are creating a canvas for ink,
crayon, paint, glitter and glue.

Remember, cooks are descendants
of wild women and paper. Write
down that secret from last night's
dream the mirror whispered to you.
Send your partner a hand-made
Valentine in July because she is
who she is and you cook for her
and make paper lovingly.

And when you are quiet in your
hammock, smile as you consider
the meal you will dish up this
evening; how you will caress
and be caressed by paper.

ODE TO THE FEMALE BODY

Ronna Magy

for this body
for these mounds of women flesh
for the way breasts rise and fall on the bones
for the lungs
for the taking of breath
for the way the back bends down generations
for the reach of these arms

for women's fingers grasping the pins
smells of fresh sheets billowing
post world war days
for mother and grandmother's hands
wringing pillow cases and towels
for women's hands
gripping wicker baskets
drawstring bags
clasping pins
for wooden pieces
fastening life into place
cotton house dresses
breathing post industrial air

ANNIVERSARY

EJ Hicks

Stuck between the pages of a hotel bible
      in central Illinois,

next to verse twenty-two in chapter
      eighteen of Leviticus,

is a sheet of paper torn from a half-empty
      notepad, adorned

with the messy scrawl of young lovers.
      It reads:

"Two dykes stayed here & loved each other
      all night long."

BAD LESBIAN

Tate

Bad Lesbian, you ain't gold star
Bad Lesbian, you're not too cool to dance in lesbian bars
Bad Lesbian, you own one flannel you may have thrown away
Bad Lesbian, you never "came out" to anyone, grew up in the
                                                golden age of gay
Bad Lesbian, your hair is dyed and long
Bad Lesbian, you used to not like Tegan and Sara songs
Bad Lesbian, no rugby, no softball
Bad Lesbian, too fearing of commitment to U-Haul, passing
                                                heterosexual
Bad Lesbian, don't like enough raw vegetables
Bad Lesbian, Jenny Schecter was your favorite character of all
Bad Lesbian, and don't even get me started on not knowing
                                                until college
Bad Lesbian, you don't drive a Subaru
Bad Lesbian, hadn't shopped at REI 'til twenty-two
Bad Lesbian, you've had acrylic nails
Bad Lesbian, the in-your-face nature of your gayness fails
Bad Lesbian, never thought twice about sleepovers with girls,
                                                and you played fucking doctor
Bad Lesbian, you're a gawker
Bad Lesbian, someone stop her
Bad Lesbian, someone stop her,
Bad Lesbian!

MARLBORO MENTHOL LIGHTS

Tate

after Natalie Diaz

She lines her lips parallel
to the burn ring like a cellist

knowing exactly how to hold the bow without tape
But it's not effortless

She's like a dog circling to get comfy
chasing her tail to escape the wind

She traces an invisible telephone cup with her hand
like she's shouting across the room inward

She'll do it again to another cigarette
to suck light into mine

Her goosebumps become speed bumps when she
thinks of our kids running toy cars over my baby bump,

one day,
and then she hands over

her favorite filter
I can't wait to quit together

WE ARE NOT SISTERS

Suzanne DeWitt Hall

We stopped for gas
on a winding Kentucky two-lane
beneath a canopy of Spanish moss
where winter-gray kudzu
awaited spring
to resume its consuming
of barns and buildings
trees and tension lines
anything vertical
a target for destruction.

Should we pretend we are sisters?
The vertical trajectory of our love
a threat
to the insidious increase of demands
about genitals
pronouns
skin color
faith or lack of it
country of origin.

The gray-haired gas keep's dialect
scared me;
its twang shocking
only a few hours from home.
He owned the place
and waited, bored
to assess those who entered.

Should we pretend we are sisters?

A young attendant also stood waiting
tongs ready to grasp
hotdogs and breakfast sandwiches
differently bored
nervous
straight black hair shining
brown skin surprising
in the vast whiteness.
So maybe it was silly
to ask the question:

Should we pretend we are sisters?

The women's restroom
could service two
as long as you were close:
mother and toddler
aunt and niece
sisters.
There were no stalls
two toilets perched
in vulnerable nakedness
on the pissy expanse of tile.

Should we pretend we are sisters?

Twin silver bullets were pulled up next door
gleaming beneath the draping moss
horses hidden inside
grateful like us
for the reprieve from the road
but like us questioning
the safety of the stop

sniffing the air
and wondering.

Should we pretend we are sisters?

I small talked the gas keep
assessing the likeliness of his stance
on two people who were not sisters
and told him about the roadside rodeo
taking place next door.
"That's my lot!" he said
annoyed that they'd encamped
without permission
then stomped off to check out the action.

Young people footworked
around the cracked pavement
spinning ropes above their cowboy hats
tossing them toward
a horned creature
made of aluminum
and blue fabric.
Capturing the thing with a swish
and a tug
while an older man tossed instructions.

"I guess they ain't hurtin nothin."
the gas keep said
hotdog youth watching
silent
leery
relieved.
I went outside
and filled the tank.

eager to drive away
from a place where we had to wonder:

Should we pretend we are sisters?

A place where
White-haired white men
issued rules
about how to best capture life
regulate truth
order the world
keep the universe from shaking apart
at threats like my spouse and I
stopping to pee
and asking:

Should we pretend we are sisters?

HORIZONTAL HOSTILITY/SISTER SABOTEUR
Roberta Arnold

Inside the D train, the squeal of metal on metal assaulted my ears like screeching chalk on a blackboard. Bean, Shona, and Tracy sat together against the side wall, facing into the car and I sat facing backwards against the window. At nine-twenty pm, we were worn out and heading home from our Women's Shelter planning meeting. Stacy had brought a pizza from John's on Bleecker and Shona had made a jug of her delicious green and black tea. Between the cheese and caffeine alternately slowing and stimulating our brains, we had finally patched together a fundraising outline and strategy, and now we were headed across town to take various trains home from the West Side. All early risers to work the next day.

I looked around: the train was empty except for a young woman sitting opposite on a window seat. Headphone wires dangled like thin branches to her shoulders, leg crossed at the ankle, feet in red high tops resting on the opposite seat. She was munching on one of her long pale fingers, a clear lip gloss smudge under her lower lip like the remnants of an oily snack. At first her face appeared shuttered, but every now and then it morphed into elastic facial expressions: an irreverent toothy grins, a mocking frown, eyeballs widening, an eyebrow shooting up to hide the silver eyebrow ring lodged in one corner. She was either reading or fast tapping her cell phone screen. She paid no attention to us as we threw our words out over the roaring train.

"C'mon, Bean, we're talking about Lu, here! She's been with us for four years! Do you really think an FBI agent would bother wasting all that time—on us?"

Bean shifted and smiled, reminding me of Wig, my tabby, with that percipient all-knowing grin.

I shook my head. "We're not even doing anything subversive for fuck's sake!"

I sat up and scooted forward on the slick metal seat, re-planting my feet firmly on the gyrating floor. Looking first at Bean's discerning eyes, then, thoughtlessly, checking my reflection in the soot-encrusted window, my head spun as subway girders, at breakneck speed, passed in front of me.

"Think about it, Mar, this happens all the time in political groups—why do you always question me, dammit, it's so annoying!" Bean sat up on the fiberglass seat, ankle across kneecap, chest thrust forward, hands grabbing the seat edge opposite me, flaring eyes the color of molasses lit up by the sun.

I don't know why I persisted—genetic oppositional defiant disorder?—but I did.

"Lu's so reliable and one of the most level-headed when it comes to dealing with abusers. Everyone else in our group, including me, gets hot-headed. Plus, she makes me laugh…"

Bean was shaking her head up and down in fierce agreement or disagreement—I couldn't figure which, her golden-sulfur eyes sizzling like firework sparklers. She said, "Yeah, that's what they do: blend and assert themselves until we are brainwashed—and *then* they sabotage!" Bean had a voice like a South Bronx smoker, the perfect blend of rasp and twang.

"Paranoid a little, Bean?" Shona jumped in, her wide infectious grin wiping away any hostility from the statement. Shona was wearing steel-tipped engineer boots, overalls, and a thin turquoise Indian print shirt showing off her glowing gingerbread skin. Her feelings were hard for me to read. Except when she implemented her forbidding tone when talking to abusers who came to the shelter. I almost pitied the men who tried to get past Shona standing Sentinel.

Tracy said, "It ain't paranoia if they're really out to get ya!" Knocking a shoulder against Bean in camaraderie. Tracy had a knack for bonding skills.

Bean rubbed her palms together like she was washing them. "Listen up, different subject, I was at the bookstore Saturday, watching Cara, the owner, adding a shelf for *gay men*. On the bulletin board she tacks something about a guy's meeting *inside* the bookstore, like an AA meeting–"

"It was a *sex addicts* anonymous meeting!" Shona roared.

"Yeah, right–a sex addicts meeting of MEN—at OUR bookstore!"

"Ok, ok, Cara opened up Atlantis Books to include self-help meetings—is that such a bad thing?" I squirmed in my seat, knowing where this was going, feeling like I was swimming against the tide.

Bean threw up her hands. "Wait, wait,—let me finish, will ya?" She shot me an exasperated look.

The three of us all chimed in at once: "Go ahead, Bean!"

"Thanks," Bean continued, taking the moment in with admirable butch pride. "So, one thing led to another. Cara tells me and Jesse she's having trouble making enough to survive from the money women contribute in sales. She mentions the flack she's getting from letting men into the bookstore then, and then–get this—she smirks!"

"Oh, no!–not the smirk!?!" Tracy did her famous eye-roll and we all laughed. Tracy has a natural deadpan delivery, her flexible body stopping at her face which sits like a totem on her head, almost wooden, except for those expressive green eyes which don't miss a trick.

"Yup!–I'm tellin' ya, that Cara is no pushover–she smirked, and then, then she does this quick hand wave up in the air, dismissive-like."

"When was the last time you bought something there?"

"Mara, just cause I don't give money doesn't mean I don't support her. And if you don't stop interrupting, I've gotta hand wave just for you!" Bean threw me a quick wink.

Flustered now, my words rushed out: "Ok, ok–all ears!"

"Yeah, right–well…" Bean gave me a pitying smile and continued, "Jesse runs over to the Women's Coffeehouse and tells everyone what has just transpired: the whole shebang: the smirk, the hand wave, the men's sex group. Long story short, the Coffeehouse Collective is demonstrating on Cornelia & 7th, right outside the bookstore, signs protesting classism, sexism.… Chanting, flyers handed out to boycott." Bean stops short, looking over at Tracy whose head was shaking, her short curls twirling in pinwheels, mouth firmly clamped close, waiting for Bean to get it.

"Oh, oh yeah, right, NOT boycott, *SISTERCOTT.*" Bean nodded acknowledgement to Tracy. "Our sisters are *sister*-cotting the bookstore. And I quote Flo: "As long as we're into piranha-ism and horizontal hostility, honey, we ain't going to get nowhere!" Bean beams and then lowers her head, continuing, "I got a call from Cara at 8:15 last night, she said it looks like they'll have to close. The boy–er, sister-cott thing pushed her over. So. We will be one less bookstore. The only one in my neighborhood!" Bean threw her hands over her face while Tracy and Shona hugged her from either side.

I leaned forward and squeezed Bean's kneecap, peering up to read between the fingers stretched over her eyes. Bean's eyes had stopped flailing, but still conveyed anguish. I wanted to wrap my arms around her and stroke the back of her head.

The train had stopped ratcheting back and forth and was doing its usual ear-piercing, brake-screeching slowdown. We were entering the oncoming station. West Fourth. Our stop. We got up in a jumble of bodies and colors: short, tall, thin, fat, white, black. Heading through the swishing rubber edges of the automatic doors together, I shot a glance over at the young woman wearing headphones. She was still oblivious to us.

Loping up the stairs two at a time toward the 6th Ave exit, I wondered if it was sometimes best to shut my mouth and keep my head down when these sister-to-sister battles erupted, or to speak my truth even if it meant knocking down another sister stronghold? I couldn't help thinking that if there was a sister saboteur among us, she wouldn't have had to do much. Even without her input, we're quick to pounce. Like my habit of interrupting. *What's up with that?* I lifted my head just in time to catch Bean's latest maneuver: Hands on either side of the turnstile, long legs pulled up beneath, Bean leap frog's over the mechanical turnstile arms. I feel a flutter in my chest, like birdwings, pumping up the wind force to soar.

IN AJAR

C. LaSandra Cummings

hir a sweetness a jar
hir touch & spoonful ajar & taste

bud speckles strawberry seed
freckles like tar

hir tears & smears in a dam
in the inside of my hand

hir spreads & spreads like jam
expands on bread

or softens or blooms instead

like coffee

like spilled cake flour

CALL IT A CATCH BREATH

Mary Maxfield

Remember the shutdown?
It wasn't just the city.

My body chilled like a temple,
emptied of its hymns.
My limbs hung limp as vacant swings
or the yellow tape ringing around the playgrounds.
Caution: this hollowness is now all I know
to hold.

In Italy, neighbors sung across balconies,
built harmonies that filled whole blocks.
Meanwhile, I could barely talk.
I muted myself for a meeting,
but the silence stuck so readily,
it weighed so heavily,
it built a home in me.
I sealed the window to the my balcony
until I couldn't hear even the birds.

For two years – two years? –
nothing stirred.

Regardless of whether we fell sick,
this virus pierced us like a shattered rib.
It knocked the wind from our lungs,
stunned us, voices frozen,
faces blank as the marquee
outside the movie theater,
announcing: nothing.

Now playing: nothing
This week: nothing
and this week: nothing
and this weak

        -ness calcified inside us.
Fatigue flowered like a fungus,
a network of rotten blossoms
blotting our hearts, our guts, our breath.
Even the luckiest among us
couldn't escape this death fully,
couldn't sidestep the way energy
leaked from our bodies like air
hissing through a hole.

When the time came to return I'd lost
even the nerve
that knew to miss you.
Even my muscle memory had amnesia.
My body was a tin man I couldn't oil-can
back to humanity.
Behold what's left of me:
just this rusty armor
just stiff joints

just meaning hovering like breath,
evaporating in front of me.
I couldn't see the point, only the risk.

I would've missed how much I've missed
the way my name moistens your lips,
the way you gripped my gaze like a fist,
held it with firmness for weeks
until we could finally touch each other
skin to skin.

I didn't know how much I'd suffocated
'til you leaned in, said, listen—
if you can't remember how to breathe,
just sing with me.
Sing with me.

For the first time in two years,
I remembered those balconies in Italy.
I opened my mouth fully,
my voice shaky as a sob.
Silence strangled the phrases.
My lungs insisted on unwritten rests.
I said, I can't do this.
You said, you can't do this alone.

Every song needs more than one note
Every chorus needs a crowd of throats
That's why they call them catch breaths
All music is a relay
A torch pressed from my chest into yours

So you still feel empty.
That only gives the echo space in you to soar
until it finds me.

Sing softly,
sorrowfully,
sing your uncertain elegy—
sing anything,
just sing with me
until our heartbeats drum in unison:
You and I,
we're still alive.

Remember,
sometimes,
when the world takes your breath away
it gives you back a song.

LESBIAN LITERATURE IN GREECE

Vagia Kalfa [Noa Tinsel]

Modern Greek lesbian literature gained some visibility during 1910-1930. During that time, original Greek works and translations of European works were published in the literary magazines Alexandrian Art and Letters, in Alexandria, where a lively community of Greek poets and writers had been formed. The works that were published tin these journals were considered immoral, even pornographic, and were marginalized in Greece. Among them, were Myrtiotissa's poems, the poem "To a Lady" by Galateia Kazantzaki, and the translation of Pierre Louys' "Songs of Bilitis." "How the Girls Mourned Sappho When She Fell In Love With Alcaeus", the only lesbian poem of Varnalis, a writer well-known in Greece for his communist ideas and Voutyras' short-story "When the Flowers Bloom" were also published there. In the latter, a disfigured, mentally-ill and sexually oppressed man who lives in the margins of society, as it is the case with the majority of Voutyras' characters, is stalking two women while they are making love in the woods and interrupts them, demanding to participate. He ends up falling off a cliff while cursing them. The short-story, which is the first one in modern Greek literature to narrate a lesbian love scene explicitly, is problematic not only in terms of how it constructs lesbians but also for the way it constructs non-hegemonic masculinities. On the one hand, lesbians seem to exist only to arouse men who feel entitled to having sex with them, since without their penis their sexual intercourse is considered incomplete. On the other hand, men should display signs of "healthy" -that is heteronormative- sexuality to be considered normal. Those who do not are considered ill and the ill (the disabled and the disfigured among them) are desexualized. Even worse, the lust of the disfigured is punished with death as if it is unimaginable for him to desire and be desired back (1).

In Greece, lesbian literature during that period was primarily written by cis heterosexual men who saw lesbians as part of the margin, along with prostitutes, drug dealers, homeless and prisoners. As such, they were often being romanticized as in need to be saved, while they were not perceived as autonomous beings who could actually desire other women. Reflecting society, where women remained for the most part uneducated, confined in the domestic sphere, performing their duties as nurturing mothers, faithful wives and good Christians, these works reproduced stereotypes from the psychiatric discourse and sexology about female homosexuality and restored heterosexuality, while allowing heterosexual men to peek through the keyhole. Among other things, indicative of men's fear of uncontrolled female sexuality (as opposed to the regulated sexuality of the wife), the lesbian was a prostitute (Bourlekis, Kalonaios, Pikros) who had an affair with another prostitute only to end it when the true loved arrived, a man who married her and allowed her to ascend financially, socially and morally. Others, echoing Ellis' theory as well as the construction of lesbianism by European writers of the late 19th century, saw lesbians as victims of feminist propaganda (Saravas) or based on Ulrich's theory, as hermaphrodites (Seferis), mannish (Politis) or, even, evil witches who seduced innocent heterosexual women (Theotokas). By being constructed as infectious, corrupted, deviant, and tormented, lesbians ultimately assuaged men's fears rather than challenged middle-class moral values (2).

Given the gender-based division of space, entering the public sphere as a woman was demonized and being a female writer raised suspicions about her morality and gender. The critics, who were mostly male, served as gatekeepers and applied double standards in their evaluations of literary works of their time, confining women to their place. Expecting them to write "melancholic" and "dreamy" works and accusing them of not being true to themselves in life and art whenever they violated gendered expectations, these critics treated transgressive works of art as a proof of women's lack of talent (3).

Despite these, a series of women wrote defiantly. Some wrote love poems that challenged patriarchy, setting aside idealized and desexualized representations of eternal love and foregrounding desire and writing about sex and the body. Some poems were lesbian either openly or in a way that can be read as such. Apart from Rita Boumi-Pappa (who, following her marriage, revised her first lesbian collection to be read as heterosexual) and Myrtiotissa (whose writing gradually diminished the lesbian element) who wrote explicitly lesbian poetry, several female poets addressed their beloved in feminine terms, utilizing abstract feminine nouns that allow for ambiguity ("Optasia" [Vision] by Rita Segkopoulou, "Thymisi" [Memory] by Fili Vatidou, "Anagni" [Not Innocent] by Olga Vatidou) or used verbs and adverbs instead of nouns and adjectives to avoid grammatical gender declarations ("Thimasai?" [Do You Remember?] by Olga Vatidou). Even explicitly lesbian love poems are desexualized in Departments of Modern Greek Literature in Greece (this is the case with gay poetry as well). For instance, Chatzivogiatzi, in her PhD thesis, refers to the poems "Thelo" [I Want] by Antoniadi and "Intermedium" by Sfakianaki but as fantasies, the externalization of which was permitted thanks to the feminist movement of the time. However, whether such an approach reflects reality is a question.

In 1929, Dora Rosetti published the autobiographical prose I Eromeni Tis [Her Beloved] which was reissued only in 2005 by Christina Dounia. The work was significant for various reasons, including openly naming the relationship between the two main characters as such and daring to envision a happy ending for them. Rosetti entrusted her work to the editors Tsoukalas and Simiriotis, asking them to make the necessary adjustments to prevent her and her former lover, who were the main characters of the story, from being identified. However, they failed to do that, causing turmoil in the lives of the two women. Rosetti and her ex's husband ended up buying up the copies from bookstores, with her setting them on fire (4).

During the military Junta in Greece (1967-1974), fundamental human and political rights were suspended, the communist party was divided, communists and generally those who opposed the dictatorial regime were imprisoned and tortured, sparking great anti-dictatorial protests (the attempted murder of Papadopoulos by Panagoulis in 1968, the Navy Movement as well as the occupation of Law and Polytechnic School of Athens in 1973). Under those circumstances, every organized women's movement was silenced except some charitable associations in the province and those which were oriented to Greek-Orthodox propaganda. Needless to say that during that period, when the triptych fatherland-religion-family was propagandized, homosexuality was chased — only in case of gay men, though. The absence of a legal framework for lesbians reflects the myth of the virtuous Greek woman, a myth that is predominantly white and bourgeois. Already in the European colonized space, working-class women were accused of crimes against purity, while African American women were believed to be more prone to homosexuality due to their supposedly enlarged clitorises.

Loukas Theodorakopoulos, a prominent gay poet, a leading figure of AKOE [Gay Liberation Movement of Greece] and founder of the LGBTQ+ journal Amfi [Bi] chronicles several homophobic incidents that took place during that time in his book Keadas: To Chroniko Mias Poliorkias [Keadas: Chronicle of a Siege]. One such incident that is worth mentioning is police's raid on a house gay party and the leakage of the guests' information to the press, which portrayed the party as an orgy, sparking moral panic (5). A similar violation of personal data occurred, albeit on a smaller scale, in 2003 when the police raided on the gay club Spices in Athens, seized the organizers' laptops, arrested random customers, and leaked their information to the press, which, this time, presented them as pedophiles and traffickers of child pornography (6). In the aftermath, a man committed suicide inside the building of Attica Police Headquarters. Public humiliation as a means of keeping the "good" Greek body "pure" and expelling the foreign/other is a common bourgeois practice in the country. In 2012 the Minister of Health of that time, Andreas Loverdos, issued a sanitary ordinance that stigmatized 27 HIV+ female drug addicts as national enemies, who worked in the sex industry and intentionally transmitted the virus. The women were forced to blood testing and sent to prison for a year despite the fact that the allegations were proved invalid, while their data were leaked to the press, leading one of them to commit suicide.

Following the fall of Junta, the feminist movement gained momentum in the country, as feminist press was on the rise (7) and women's organizations were formed initially within the framework of trade unions and then as alternative groups, gradually creating an autonomous feminist space. Marriage was challenged and found a source of women's oppression, as they were starting to claim their bodily autonomy and sexual freedom. Nighttime protests against rape and gender-based violence were organized, while marches and counter-rallies were held to claim and win a series of rights, such as the reform of Family Law (abolition of dowry, elimination of distinction between children born within and outside of marriage, civil marriage, and legal recognition of gender equality) and the legalization of abortion. These efforts faced tremendous opposition from anti-abortion religious organizations, as well as the teaching and research staff of the Medical School of the Aristotle University of Thessaloniki, while attempts were made to manipulate public opinion through the screening of anti-abortion films by the Movement for the Right to Life.

Several lesbian groups were formed during this time. However, they counted only a few members and did not have their own space. They coexisted, instead, at times with feminist groups and, at other times, with gay groups, without fully identifying with neither of those. During this decade, friendship among lesbians was based on shared sexuality (which later gave way to the formation of lesbian and gay families) and was particularly highlighted when there was a rupture with the family of origin. However, sexual preference alone was not sufficient to maintain these friendships, leading the groups to fall apart. A prerequisite for such friendships was coming out, derived from the West and rooted in confessional mechanisms (Catholic dogma, psychoanalysis). To this day, coming out, is considered a central liberating mechanism, and remains theoretically and politically unchallenged (8).

The 80s and 90s in Greece included a moral panic caused by the HIV/AIDS crisis, the success of the second-wave feminism, and the Greece's entrance to the European Union, which forced the country to take action in terms of gender-based inequalities and violence, the mainstream press, capitalizing on male fears, constructed typologies of lesbians (the "outed" and the "closeted", the "feminine" and the "mannish"), speculated the causes of lesbianism (often attributing it to trauma, especially sexual abuse), and generally scrutinized women to terrorize them. Several LGBTQ+ journals were released with Lavrys and Madam Gou being exclusively lesbian. Lavrys viewed lesbians as a third gender, adopting Wittig's approach and raised the issue of female sexuality and bodily autonomy in patriarchy, condemning butches and pornography as inherently patriarchal. Madam Gou, circulating during a decade when feminism was considered outdated and intellectually bankrupt, and the panic over Macedonia and the crisis in Imia, the opening of borders, and the entry of immigrants was pervasive, attempted to connect lesbian feminism of the country to the international movement and criticized the LGBTQ+ claims for marriage as homonormativity (9).

Neoliberalism and consumerism permeating Greek society during the 90s were also reflected in magazines like KLIK, which snubbed the lower social classes, mocked "Balkan" forms of entertainment, and sought to make lesbians (especially those from the working class and with a "masculine" appearance, wearing checkered shirts and cowboyish boots) conform to Western - and urbanized – femininity (10). In the meantime, Eressos (11), which had its own unique story, declined. Out of need for women-only spaces, Cyberdyke Parties, were organized in Athens by Maria Cyber, who until now, writes about trans men, butch lesbians, drag king culture, and lesbian pornography (12). Despite the intense activism of the time, this work is not reflected, as far as we know, in literature (this is not the case with gay literature which is present throughout this century), with the exception of the work of Hara Hristara.

REFERENCES

(1), (2) Vogiatzi, P. (2019), Αναπαραστάσεις της Γυναικείας Ομοφυλοφιλίας στην Ελληνική Λογοτεχνία των Αρχών του 20^{ου} αιώνα, University of Ioannina (master dissertation)

(3)Chatzivogiatzi, O. (2018). Αναζητώντας τη Γυναικεία Ποίηση στα Χρόνια του Μεσοπολέμου. Μια Καταγραφή της Εργογραφίας αλλά και της Κριτικής Πρόσληψης των Ελληνίδων Ποιητριών, National and Kapodistrian University of Athens (PhD thesis).

(4) Bakopoulou, E. (2006), «Παραλειπόμενα Ντόρας Ρωζέττη», Odos Panos, 133

(5) See also: Antonopoulos, T., «Μια Πρωτοφανής Επιχείρηση Αρετής Σε Ιδιωτικό Πάρτυ την Περίοδο της Χούντας», lifo, 28/7/2019, https://www.lifo.gr/lgbtqi/mia-protofanis-epiheirisi-aretis-se-idiotiko-parti-tin-periodo-tis-hoyntas.

(6), (9), 10) Simati, A. (2022), Οι Νταλίκες και τα Γυναικάκια τους. Θηλυκοί Ανδρισμοί και Πολιτικές της Γυναικείας Ομοερωτικής Επιθυμίας, Futura.

(7) Vagionaki, M. (2006), Τα Φεμινιστικά και τα Γυναικεία Εντυπα στην Ελλάδα (1975-2000). Θεματολογία, Ιδεολογικοί Προβληματισμοί και Εκπαιδευτικές Αντανακλάσεις, Aristotle University of Thessaloniki (master dissertation); Sioziou, D. (2012), Εναλλακτικά Μέσα, Φύλο και Κοινωνικά Κινήματα στην Ελλάδα:

από το Ριζοσπαστικό Φεμινισμό στο Queer, Panteion University (master dissertation).

(8) Kantsa, V. (2012), «Ορατά Αόρατες/ Αόρατα Ορατές: Δύο Οψεις της Λεσβιακής Παρουσίας στην Ελλάδα» In Apostoleli, A., Chalkia, A. (eds.), Σώμα, Φύλο, Σεξουαλικότητα. ΛΟΑΤΚ Πολιτικές στην Ελλάδα, Plethron, p.p. 29-52.

(11)Kokkini, M, «Η Λεσβιακή Ιστορία της Ερεσού», *lifo*, 15/8/2022, https://www.lifo.gr/lgbtqi/i-lesbiaki-istoria-tis-eresoy

(12) Maria Cyber, «Οι Λεσβίες της Αθήνας Είχαν τη Δική τους Ιστορία: η Μαρία Cyber την Καταγράφει» *lifo*, 16/6/2019, https://www.lifo.gr/lgbtqi/oi-lesbies-tis-athinas-eihan-ti-diki-toys-istoria-i-maria-cyber-tin-katagrafei

PHOTOGRAPH BY RIPLEY BUTTERFIELD

ALEPH

Aviva Betzer

I open my mouth and nothing comes out.
I am all mouth, binging on seedless
Grapes. I open my eyes, it is dark.
I stick to routine: when guests arrive,
I serve chocolates.
I kiss my niece on her birthday.
Nothing comes out because someone stole my mouth.
A man came over, pried open
The front door and took it.
Now my mouth's gone,
My eyes watch carefully as you storm
Through the empty room.
I howl the magnificent void—

BEIT, THE SECOND LETTER

Aviva Betzer

Nothing can save me from this polluted body.
Limbs and commas flail like a howling wind
Through the house. Beit is the second letter
In the Hebrew alphabet. Beit is for house
Although once it was much simpler—
There was a father and a mother.
Once I was young and emaciated,
It was all about slamming doors and yelling.
The rain punctured my lungs
As I ran down the road.
No more. I sit on a park bench,
I sit on a couch
In my therapist's waiting room.
You were right: my mouth opens
and it sounds like a catastrophe.

AT THE PRISON CAMP IN ALABAMA

René Baek Goddard

"In recognition of loving lies an answer to despair."
–Audre Lorde

There are blackbirds everywhere. They build nests in the awnings out of clay, and every week the courtyard orderlies knock them down with mop handles. The birds fly wildly, in circles and zig-zags, like they're lost, and perch on the beams where their homes used to be. They leave and come back with mouthfuls of clay to rebuild again, and they do this dance every week, over and over again.

When they take to the skies, they look like tiny black specks on a beautiful pink and lavender Alabama sunset. The sky here is breathtaking. It's easily the most vibrant, beautiful thing about this place, where everyone wears grey and green, where us inmates live in concrete, metal, and rubber—at least I get to step outside and see southern skies, baby blues turn into purples and fuschias and crimsons speckled with white clouds and evening stars.

I wonder if those blackbirds migrate, too. I wonder if they would go as far as Texas, where my Angel is locked up. I wonder if they would pass over Arkansas, where I fell in love with her, where we built the first thing we ever called home.

The portrait of our queer southern life had so many colors. Cruising through Little Rock—Angel driving with her knees while rolling a blunt (don't try this), Smino and Kari Faux and Ari Lennox and the droning of cicadas serenading our night drive. At home, my cat hissing at her dog, the pitter-patter of claws scrabbling across the floor. Slamming screen doors and the smell of something spicy cooking on the stove. Bonfires and cookouts and mosquito bites in hot, sticky southern summers. Angel picking me up at the strip club I worked at—marked by a lone neon sign off the highway—with a bag of Shark's Chicken and Fish waiting in the seat for me. Marching together on the Little Rock capitol building in protest of some new backwards conservative law—our numbers few, but our voices loud. Friday nights in a tiny, cigarette-smoke drenched dive.

Picking up Sprites and Andy Capp's Hot Fries at the Kum-n-Go, hand-in-hand, a flaming butch and femme flagging in everybody's faces, ignoring the scowls and glares. Often a man would be bold enough to catcall me, and you bet Angel would be there, right up in his face. And sometimes a man had something to say about Angel's seemingly indecipherable gender presentation, and you know my mouth would be ready to fire back. Because if we don't got each other, who does?

Most of our friend group in Little Rock came from trailer parks and middle-of-nowhere towns, from working class families or families on welfare or family members struggling with addiction, bouncing in and out of jail. Our friends (and sometimes ourselves) were housing insecure and U-Hauling from one partner to the next. Angel spent years as a teen couch-hopping and street-living. In the queer south, it's more rare to have a stable family who accepted you, than to be one of many kicked or forced out of their homes. When Lucie's Place, Little Rock's nonprofit for LGBT youth where I worked as a resident assistant, suddenly closed its only shelter, Angel and I found ourselves taking in several former residents in our own homes.

Southern queer life is intimate by nature, out of necessity—because if we don't got each other, who does?

When Angel and I moved to Chicago years later, we found ourselves in culture shock. The Chicago northside-centered queer spaces we found ourselves in were full of suburbanites from upper middle class to wealthy families, college students with financial safety nets, microcelebrities and social media influencers. It was a different world than the scrappy and down-to-earth southern queer community we had grown to love in Little Rock.

"Isn't it crazy we met in Little Rock of all places?" she would joke. And it's true—winds of history so much bigger than the two of us swept both of us here from half a world away, to this unlikeliest of places. U.S imperialism and neocolonialism created the conditions for both of our migrations, another meaningful connection threading our lives together.

As a military brat who grew up moving often and far, I always believed we have two birthplaces: the one where we came out of the womb, and the one where we truly found ourselves. Both places leave their mark on us.

Angel was born in Chile and brought to Arkansas at seven years old when her family searched for better opportunities. She grew up in a Black and Latino neighborhood in Little Rock nearly all her life. I was born to a Korean mother and American father in Mississippi, but I spent ten years of my life in a military town in South Korea before returning to the American south and settling in Little Rock.

I think one of the reasons Angel and I were drawn to each other was because we possessed these dualities—an American southern ruggedness and individuality, intertwined with a "foreign" cultural openmindedness and collectivist spirit.

One of the first times I really spoke to Angel was at a banner-making and letter-writing party at her house. We got together to make signs for a protest and write letters to incarcerated queer people through an organization called Black and Pink.

I liked that beneath Angel's charismatic masculinity and butch appearance, a shy sweetness peeked out. As an introverted person myself, I felt at ease around her, despite her demeanor that some called aggressive or loud. We talked about everything—about how Leslie Feinberg and *Stone Butch Blues* changed our lives, our love of books, our faraway motherlands, our immigrant family members, our desire for more internationalism in the movement here. I loved her militancy and commitment to revolution. I loved how our lesbian gender performances complemented and contrasted each other, how we played inside the roles and loved to play outside them, too.

I loved how we didn't conform to people's ideas and expectations of us, how they called us "heteronormative" and we'd laugh like our butchness and femmeness were an inside joke—and they just didn't get it.

"People look at us and think they know who Leslie is at a glance. Then they think they know who I am because I am with her," Minnie Bruce Pratt wrote in "Sir and Ma'am" in *Sinister Wisdom* 132. "And they don' they don't they don't know anything at all because every moment we ourselves are making it up, back and forth. How do we do this genderfuck sex together, the kiss and the sorrow, the laundry and the travel, up the back staircase of what we've been taught to do."

Angel became my steel-covered velvet, and I became her velvet-covered steel. Strength and hardness and softness and lushness inside each other. Beyond roles, beyond play-acting.

But with small, intimate communities, there is a double-edged sword. Much like prison life, southern queer life can make you feel like you're always under a microscope. It can be beautiful that we all know each other so intimately, and it can also be exhausting and frustrating.

Angel and I were already in relationships when we met. There was history. Our falling in love—and the recklessness with which we went about it—reopened old wounds, dredged up past conflicts, and hurt people important to us. We moved in a small pond and made waves that not everyone liked. At first, it seemed nobody wanted us to be together. And after years of reflection, I understand why.

I think if I hid this part of our love story, I wouldn't do it justice. Just like Angel and I, just like the histories that brought us together, and just like our dirty south, our love story is rough around the edges, imperfect, and not always pretty to look at. And I don't think I would have it any other way. We would not be who we are or carry this resilience had we not fucked up and learned from it. The beautiful parts would not shine so brightly if it weren't for the grimy bits. That's queer southern love.

And I loved our militance, our boldness, our mutual willingness to take risks. I *loved* being with someone as fiery as me, because the heat never dies down. But sometimes it burns.

In the summer of 2020, the whole country burned for George Floyd. While we were marching, we spotted cops roughing up a man in an alley. Recklessly, we ran towards them. The cops shoved my face into the concrete when they arrested us. That was first time I went to jail with Angel.

Then, six months later in December of 2020, we were both arrested by ATF for federal arson, conspiracy, and possession of a destructive device.

Almost exactly three years later, Angel and I were finally sentenced in the historic Little Rock 9 courtroom, to eighteen months in federal prison. We held each other while the prosecutor walked by. He refused to make eye contact with us.

"We'll be okay," Angel kept whispering.

Now that Angel and I are both sitting inside the prison walls, I find an irony to that old memory of us meeting at a Black and Pink letter-writing party. My friend always liked to tell me that my life has "bookends."

Inmates in federal custody at different institutions are prohibited from speaking to each other. But that doesn't mean people don't do it. There's always a way.

"Now even the United States of America don't wanna see us together," Angel would say, and I laugh. I loved that she was always full of jokes, even in situations like this.

Valentine's Day in a women's prison was agony. I was surrounded by couples giving each other Honey Buns, jailhouse cheesecakes made of creamer and pudding and vanilla wafers, paper roses dipped in red and green Kool-Aid, elaborate pop-up cards and crocheted teddy bears, and all I could think about was Angel.

So I made her a comic strip of our adventures, using my cheap little Bic pen from commissary and letter paper. At the end, I drew a picture of us on our trip to Puerto Rico, before we surrendered to prison. We camped out in the jungle, and one night a lightning bug flew in and circled above us. We liked to say it was Angel's papi, who had passed years ago, blessing us with good luck.

On my drawing of this memory, I wrote: "I've had my best days and worst days with you. I wouldn't have wanted to spend them with anybody else. I love you, mi media naranjita." My half-orange. I had started calling her this when she told me that Spanish-speakers say this to their partners, because no two oranges are the same, and so each half only has one match.

She said she put the comic up in her locker. She carries a picture of me in her pocket, tapes it to her bat when she plays softball in the yard, shares coffee with me in the morning, tells me good night every evening.

"I'm in high rises so I watch the Texas sun set every day and wish so hard I could share that beautiful sight with you," she wrote. "You make my life alright, no matter what's happening. I feel like you would make me forget I was in prison with the kind of love we share."

The other day, I gushed about Angel to my friends in the rec room. A girl named Mimi said, "Is she Spanish? Transgender? Cleans all the time? They call her Espinosa? I think she was my neighbor at the transfer center!"

It's got to be her. I grabbed my photo album and showed her.

"Oh yeah, that's her," Mimi laughed. "Girl, she would not shut up about you. All she would talk about all day was wanting to get to Alabama to be with her girl. One time, her cellie started talking about her own boyfriend, and Espinosa cut her off to start talkin' about you!"

I blushed while everyone laughed.

Since we've been locked up, Angel and I have read Assata and Zami, and now we are figuring out what to read next. Even hundreds of miles away, we found a way to share books together.

There's always a way.

As I write this, I hear the blackbirds' strange, mournful chirps outside the window. Their nests are back up again.

PULPS—PAST AND PRESENT

DISCOVERING LESBIAN PULPS

Cassidy Hunt

The first time I read a pulp novel in 2015, I was fourteen, closeted and reading any book with even a hint of lesbian themes that I could find on the Kindle marketplace. I stumbled across *Odd Girl Out* by Ann Bannon for 99p. I devoured the whole book in one sitting, then immediately deleted it from my account once I was finished. Looking back, it is funny to think that the way I was reading the *Beebo Brinker* series as a closet lesbian in the 2010s was actually a reflection of the first life of lesbian pulps in the 1950s: sold for cheap in drugstores and bus terminals, hidden in the back pocket and once read, thrown away quickly to hide any evidence.

Now that I'm a fully-fledged, out-the-closet dyke, I have a collection of first and second edition lesbian pulps in my bedroom. I've collected them over the last few years; they are the pride and joy of my at-home lesbian library. I began collecting the physical copies in 2021 when lockdown reminiscence led me back to the *Beebo Brinker* ebooks still saved in my Kindle library; my love for pulps reignited. This time around, I was able to read the books with a greater affection, a much deeper understanding of their historical contexts, and a deep veneration for the historicity of lesbian culture that they preserve in their pages. At University, I read an article about lesbian pulps by Stephanie Foote, who writes that "pulps have been understood as signs of a secret history of readers, and they have been valued because they have been read. The more they are read, the more they are valued, and the more they are read...". The life cycles of these books, being read and loved by generations of lesbians one after the other, articulated to me my desire to keep on collecting these piles of beat-up, sometimes mouldy and often coffee-stained, decades-old copies of pulp novels—not just for their texts, but for their value as historic artefacts of lesbian culture.

The magic of being a lesbian, I've found, is always rooted in the community around me. As such, there's something special to me about the pulp novel which, at the time of publishing, was so threatening to own that "women hid them, burnt them, and threw them out", yet regardless were consumed in such quantities that they helped to carve a sense of self-defined lesbian identity across a generation in the US. There's an importance to me, for example, in owning two copies of Ann Banon's, *Journey To A Woman*—one first edition Gold Medal Books copy, and a second Naiad Press reprint from 1983—in showing how the production and consumption of the text changes over time. Moving from an era where pulp novels were produced cheap enough and consumed secretively enough that you could, as Ann Bannon said, "read them on the bus and leave them on the seat", to be republished twenty years later *by* lesbians, *for* lesbians shows an incredible shift in lesbian print culture. To see these books evolve from 'survival literature' - terrifying and intimidating to purchase - to becoming a beloved piece of lesbian history, read and adored with a sense of irony and affection by younger dykes today is an incredible evolution to witness.

There seems to be a slow resurgence of the pulp novel in the last few years, with Cleis Press republishing Ann Bannon's *Beebo Brinker* pulp series alongside Vin Packer's *Spring Fire.* If you look online, pulp covers are printed onto t-shirts, playing cards, cigarette cases and flasks; the staple image of modern 'dyke camp', with the lurid cover images and sensationalised taglines depicting lesbian relationships as dangerous and echoing the anxieties of the 1950s with regard to gender and sexuality. I am fascinated by this life-cycle of the pulp genre over the last seventy years, from something to be kept hidden, transformed into something to be loved and kept alive as an essential piece of our history. When I look at the pile of pulp novels on the bookshelves in my bedroom, I like to wonder who first purchased them in 1958, where they read them, how long they kept hold of them, how many other bookshelves the novel has lived on before mine; if in fifty years, these books will land in the hands of another young lesbian, and if they will wonder the same things that I do.

LESBIAN PULPS CHANGED MY LIFE
Maida Tilchen

The 1970s era of out and politicized "second wave" lesbians provided many lesbian-written books released by lesbian-owned independent publishers. But less than twenty years earlier, in the closeted, McCarthy-era 1950s, the only visibly lesbian books available were the paperback originals called "lesbian pulps." For the often-isolated lesbians then, they were a beacon that others like them existed. They told stories of lesbian romances, but the male publishers made sure the message was negative and appealing to men and homophobes. The formula plots usually ended with the butch character dead in a car crash and the femme character going back to her husband or boyfriend.

In the fall of 1972, I lived for a few months in the little rural town of Milton, Vermont, while working near Burlington. I had recently realized I was a lesbian, but I didn't know any others. I was eager

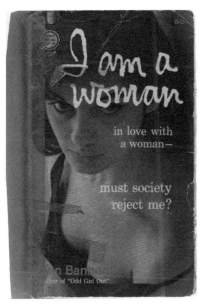

for information. My college library had only supplied a clinical book called *Changing Homosexuality in the Male* (1970).

Milton's public library was in a little old wooden house. All the books were in the small living room, where the librarian sat at a huge desk. I was browsing the unpromising shelves when I pulled out a small paperback. The title was *I am a woman, in love with a woman-- must society reject me?* by Ann Bannon.

At last, a book about lesbians! The flamboyant cover made the topic apparent and was an immediate attraction. Motivated enough to overcome my fear of exposure, I brought it to the librarian to check out. She held it up to stare closely at the cover and said, "I didn't know we had anything like that here!" That was how I began collecting lesbian books. At first, it was just the pulps, because the covers made them conspicuous.

By 1974, I was living in Bloomington, Indiana. My partner at that time, Fran Koski, and I spent most of our free hours searching for pulps at every used bookstore in the area. We hit the mother-lode at a thrift store in a huge sprawling barn. They had tens of thousands of books on long avenues of shelves over tables and in hundreds of boxes underneath. We were there nearly every weekend for a year going through it all and pulling out hundreds of pulps, priced at 10 cents each.

We read many of them and it was soon evident that the best, which were the most lesbian-identified rather than those aimed at men, were written by Ann Bannon, Valerie Taylor, and Ann Aldrich/Vin Packer (pseudonyms of Marijane Meaker). Most lesbians who have read many pulps are drawn to these writers. Something about the quality of their writing and the depth of their characters stood out.

Fran and I would go anywhere there might be used books to buy. This took us into several "adult" bookstores in rural Indiana. The customers glared at us. They did not want their "men-only" space invaded. But the proprietors had to let us in. I'm guessing they thought we might be undercover cops and they had to show there was nothing illegal. We ignored them all. Many stores had some old paperbacks, too often on a neglected bottom shelf, so our eyes were on the floor, not on whatever the men were doing.

I was working at Indiana University in a building next to Good-body Hall, which housed the Institute for Sex Research, better known as the Kinsey Institute. By a very fortunate coincidence, the job I had arbitrarily been assigned to included assisting Noretta Koertge, at that time the only out professor at the school. Noretta had the power to assure the Institute that I was a responsible researcher, so I acquired total access to the Kinsey Library. That library had been built and maintained by Jeannette Foster, who had privately published *Sex Variant Women in Literature* in 1956, the first bibliographic book on the topic. (Don't miss Joanne Passet's wonderful biography *Sex Variant Woman: The Life of Jeannette Howard Foster*). The library had a great collection of pulps, although rebound in hard covers.

Not every lesbian book had a lurid cover or title or was in paperback. If I hadn't read about *The Well of Loneliness*, I would not have recognized it in a hardcover edition. To identify lesbian books by more than obvious covers, we acquired a photocopy of the 1967 first edition of *The Lesbian in Literature: A Bibliography* by Gene Damon and Lee Stuart, published by *The Ladder*. Gene Damon was the pseudonym of Barbara Grier, editor of *The Ladder* and later owner of Naiad Press. Marion Zimmer Bradley, later famous as a fantasy novelist, developed the first mimeographed versions, called "Astra's Tower Special Leaflets #2 and #3 (1958) and they worked together on "The Checklist" (1961 and 1962). It was annotated with their A, B, C, and "T for Trash" rating system. In 1975 the second edition of *The Lesbian in Literature: A Bibliography* was published by *The Ladder*.

Fran and I were fascinated by the pulps but couldn't find out much about the authors, why they were published or how they were sold. We especially wondered about Ann Bannon, as her series of six related books told the most detailed story with continuing characters. Although lesbian-owned periodicals and small press books were starting to appear, finding pulps felt like excavating forgotten artifacts of a past world.

There was so little lesbian history available to us in the early seventies, but we knew that our experience as second-wave lesbian feminists in a Big Ten Indiana college town was very different from the closeted, butch/femme, often tragic Greenwich Village world of the pulps. Even though it was only twenty years since the earliest ones we found were published, no one else we knew valued them. Our young "second wave" lesbian friends in Bloomington would smile at the covers but weren't interested. In other contexts than the pulps, we experienced that many seventies lesbians needed to see themselves as different from the earlier generation, especially regarding the butch/femme image, which was seen as unfeminist. When we facilitated a "free university" class for the local lesbian community, everyone was insistent that our generation did not do "butch/femme." (Maybe that was because everyone was wearing overalls and flannel shirts, so their lesbian-ness wasn't doubted.)

It's not unlike how some of the current younger generation disparages my seventies generation on issues such as acceptance of transgender and non-binary identity. The young rejecting the old ways is an old story. Fortunately, there are always some young people who do want to identify and preserve our history. But for lesbians and gay men doing this in the early 1970s, there were no LGBTQ+ studies classes, journals, dissertations, or documentary movies. What we had were the pulps, time capsules buried in used bookstores.

Kate Millett, born 1934, was perhaps caught on the cusp of the older and younger generations when she wrote this in her memoir *Flying*: "What was I then, some pulp Sappho? The library of cheap paperback Lesbian affairs ... I hoarded once because they were the only books where one woman kissed another ... Really, I was ashamed of them as writing ... the cliché of their predicament, heartbroken butch murders her dog, etc. The only blooms in the desert, they were also books about grotesques." (Kate Millett, *Flying*, New York: Ballantine Books, 1974, p. 202.)

Fran and I learned about a call for articles for a special issue on lesbian literature to be in *Margins Magazine: A Review of Little Magazines and Small Press Books.* We were both aspiring writers with no idea of how to get published. But here was our chance to tell other people about the pulps. Our article "Some Pulp Sappho" (the title taken from Millet in *Flying*) summarized typical plots, with excerpts from the dialogue. It was published in August 1975, in a *Margins* issue edited by Beth Hodges, later an editor of *Sinister Wisdom*.

Our *Margins* article is usually considered the first published appreciation of the pulps by second-wave feminists. It was reprinted in *Lavender Culture*, the 1978 anthology by Karla Jay and Allen Young. When I met with Karla Jay in Greenwich Village several years later, she took me to lunch at Bagel Land—then the current state of the Stonewall Bar.

In 1975, Bloomington's LGBTQ+ activists put on the "First Midwest Gay/Lesbian Conference" in Bloomington. Leonard Matlovitch, Elaine Noble, Troy Perry, and many other nationally known celebrities spoke there. For the conference, Fran and I created a slide show mostly about the pulps, with a few other lesbian classics included. The soundtrack was four of our friends acting out the most dramatic dialogues from the pulps to go with the most outrageous cover images. For the next ten years, the slide show was shown to classes at many colleges and several conferences. I especially remember showing it to Barbara Smith's class at the University of Massachusetts, Boston.

In 1974, Fran and I attended the First Lesbian Writer's Conference, which was held in Chicago, and produced by the great organizer Marie Kuda (don't miss the biography *Kuda: Gay and Proud* edited by Tracy Baim.) Valerie Taylor, one of the three highly regarded pulp writers, was the keynote speaker. I remember squeezing into her VW bug with other "Dyke Writers" (as the conference button read) as she drove us in search of a restaurant. She told us about raising her (I think) five sons and about her anti-Vietnam War activities. At the 1975 conference, we showed our slide show. We met our role model, keynote speaker Barbara Grier, the ultimate pulp collector and publicist of pulp novels. Paula Christian, another prolific pulp writer, also spoke.

An advertisement in a lesbian periodical offered sets of back issues of *The Ladder*. Our copies arrived with a note from Barbara Grier saying it was the last set to be sold. My lesbian aunt, Helen "Ilana" Weinstock, told me that she had helped collate some of the first issues in San Francisco in 1956. (My correspondence with my aunt is in *Nice Jewish Girls: A Lesbian Anthology*.)

With my start in *Margins*, I began writing regularly for *Gay Community News* in Boston and *The Body Politic* in Toronto, two lefty feminist LGBTQ+ periodicals where women and men had equal participation. In 1978, I visited Barbara Grier and her partner Donna McBride at their home near Kansas City, to interview Barbara for *The Body Politic*. She showed me her huge book collection (which she willed to the San Francisco Public Library). She was glad that another generation was appreciating and preserving the pulps. We speculated about Ann Bannon, who despite her bestselling mid-1950s Gold Medal/Fawcett Crest lesbian pulps had never disclosed her real name or any personal information. I was surprised that even Barbara didn't know her true identity. Unfortunately, that interview was never published. It was seized in the Canadian government's notorious raid on *The Body Politic* and the Little Sisters (feminist) Bookstore in 1979. *The Body Politic* was never published again. (Anyone thinking of moving to Canada should take a good look at their "freedom of the press" protection.) I gave Joanne Passet a copy of the interview, plus told her my recollections of Barbara, for her biography *Indomitable: The Life of Barbara Grier*.

In 1979, Kate Millett gave a speech at Indiana University and then visited my home in Bloomington. (We had mutual friends). When I showed her my pulp collection, she guilt-tripped my precious copy of Ann Bannon's *Beebo Brinker* off me, saying she needed to quote from it in speeches, which she did. She also invited me to a solstice celebration weekend at her farm in Poughkeepsie.

I moved to Boston in 1980 to work on the collective staff of *Gay Community News*. At that time, I donated about a thousand books, mostly pulps, to the Lesbian Herstory Archives. Judith Schwarz, an archivist, listed them all in a bibliography entitled "The Maida Tilchen Collection." I believe the books have since been dispersed into the general collection. I am the "cover girl" for the May 24, 1980, edition of *Gay Community News*, which had an article about Bannon's writing by Andrea Freud Loewenstein. The posed photos were taken at a used bookstore. Walking through a subway station that week, I saw the cover on a newsstand.

Photo Credit: Susan Fleischmann

In 1981, Barbara Grier asked me to write the preface to the third and last edition of *The Lesbian in Literature: A Bibliography*, published by her new company Naiad Press. For reasons of cost, that edition does not include most of Barbara's "T for Trash" listings, so if you are collecting, find the earlier versions.

In 1982, Barbara had finally found Ann Bannon (a professor in Sacramento!) and was re-issuing her novels. Barbara asked me to do the first published interview with Ann. I was over the moon and of course very anxious to talk to this mythic figure. We did that interview over the phone. Ann is so gracious and delightful, and it was a pleasure. The interview was published in *Gay Community News* on January 8, 1983. (Unfortunately, the typesetter left my by-line off!) Ann and I finally met in person in 1984 at the National Women's Music Festival in Bloomington. We had lunch, took photos together, and continued our friendship.

Photo Credit: Maida Tilchen

Ann Bannon (l.), Maida Tilchen (r.)

In 1984, some Boston women adapted Beebo Brinker's story into a playscript and received Ann's permission to stage it. For about a year, we did fundraising events and the play was cast. For the Gay Pride March, we waved to the crowd riding in the vintage red Cadillac convertible of the Saints Collective (local lesbians who ran a lesbian bar), and our costumed actors presented scenes from the stage. Unfortunately, that was the high point, as the effort was ended by a conflict between the producers.

Photo Credit: Maida Tilchen

In 1995, I moderated a panel at the Outwrite Conference (a large LGBTQ+ writer's conference in Boston that was held annually for several years and produced by *Gay Community News*). Barbara Grier and Ann Bannon were panelists. At another panel later that day, I recognized Marijane Meaker (aka Ann Aldrich, Vin Packer, M.J. Meaker, M.E. Kerr, and many other pseudonyms) in the audience. I knew that she had been Ann Bannon's mentor in the world of pulp writing, but I had heard they had fallen out as friends. I hesitantly asked if they were reconnecting at this conference. She was surprised to hear that Ann was there and said they hadn't seen each other for years. I found Barbara Grier, and she took over, arranging for them to meet. I believe they did meet, but I wasn't there although I would have loved to have been a fly on the wall. Barbara never told me what occurred.

In December 2023, I sent a draft of the article you are currently reading to Ann Bannon. I wanted to make sure she was ok with the anecdote reported above. She sent me the following reply:

Photo Credit: Ann Bannon

Ann Bannon and Marijane Meaker at La Focaccia Restaurant
in Greenwich Village, June 12, 2004

"This is a lovely essay! I don't remember having a "falling out" with Marijane, but she did sort of slide out of my life for a while. She had a mad romance with Patricia Highsmith, which was destined not to last, and went back to her writing and old friends. We reconnected in later years, and I wrote a number of essays about her that she loved. I think, at the time she died, we had been set for many years in a firm friendship. We discovered that we were both grads of Big Ten universities (she: Missouri; me: Illinois) with aspirations to be writers, and of course, both wrote for the pulps. She pulled me on board by introducing me to the Editor-in-Chief at Gold Medal Books, Dick Carroll. That launched my career. So, we were intertwined over the years, often corresponded, and sang each other's praises. BTW, the beautiful girl sitting next to me at Sevilla Restaurant is my kid. While she was off to the ladies' room, and after Marijane and she had had a nice conversation, Marijane said, "Gee, I probably should have had one of my own!" Hard to believe she was wistful about having a child!"

Photo Credit: Ann Bannon

Ann Bannon's daughter, Ann Bannon, and Marijane Meaker October 1, 2006

Meeting all the Big Three—Ann Bannon, Valerie Taylor, and Marijane Meaker--I think of that as achieving the Trifecta of Lesbian Pulps! Add in Barbara Grier—is there a word for four?

In 1999, I was asked to write the entries on Ann Bannon and lesbian pulps for *The Bloomsbury Guide to Women's Literature*. When Terry Gross interviewed Ann Bannon for her radio show *Fresh Air* on December 8, 1999, she quoted from my entry, although I wasn't named. Ann Bannon has been a good luck charm for me!

The very successful 2007 off-Broadway theater production of "The Beebo Brinker Chronicles" led a new generation of Boston theater folks to stage a local production in 2011. It was a young cast, not all LGBTQ+, and they didn't know the history or context of the books. I invited the director and cast to my home to see my pulp collection and hear about the pulps. I didn't tell them my special surprise: in the middle of our meeting, my phone rang, I put it on speaker, and they heard "this is Ann Bannon, and if you have any questions about Beebo, I'd be glad to answer them." Beebo and her friends and lovers came alive when the play was presented at the Footlights Theater in Jamaica Plain for a thrilled audience.

As of 2023, I still correspond occasionally with the delightful Ann Bannon. After decades of hiding, she has become one of the most accessible lesbian celebrities. She has a great website, and a Facebook page, and can be seen in Zooms on YouTube.

Over the years, I connected with a few other pulp collectors, Robin Cohen in Denver, and Ruth Dworin in Toronto. We've done a little trading, much bragging about great finds, and shared our stories—which you can read in this issue of *Sinister Wisdom*.

I still go to many used bookstores and library book sales, but it's been years since I came across any pulps. Occasionally, friends give me the ones they have saved. I'm currently downsizing and hoping to sell my collection to a library or a buyer who will preserve it.

Collecting pulps not only gave me a way to learn about being a lesbian and lesbian history, but it also gave me many adventures and friendships, taking me from the grimy floors of "adult" bookstores to speaking in many college classes. Writing about the pulps also started my life path as a journalist and novelist and led to my proudest accomplishment: my body of published writing. My first article on pulps in *Margins* led to my hundreds of published articles in many lesbian, LGBTQ+, feminist, and Jewish periodicals; and feminist anthologies. Like Ann Bannon, I wanted to "get on board" as a writer of lesbian books: I have published two historical novels about lesbians in New Mexico in the 1920s, *Land Beyond Maps* (2009) and *She's Gone Santa Fe* (2013). Barbara Grier and Ann Bannon generously provided flattering blurbs for the back cover of *Land Beyond Maps*.

If you would like to read a lesbian pulp, a few by Ann Bannon and Marijane Meaker may be available on your local public library's eBook services, Hoopla or Libby. Each public library's collection varies. Anyone wanting to collect today should search for the lesbian independent press books of the 1970s and '80s. Daughters Incorporated and Naiad were the most prominent, but they couldn't publish every one. Many lesbian writers created their own my-book-only publishing houses to get their books out. These were printed in small quantities, weren't in libraries, and were harder to find than pulps. Unlike the pulps, these were lesbian-identified and feminist. I reviewed many in *Gay Community News* but didn't collect them. I hope my experiences inspire others to collect and preserve these.

MAUREEN C. SPEAKING WITH MAIDA TILCHEN: ON MEETING MARIJANE MEAKER

Maureen C.

Maureen C. is a long-time pulp collector who was contacted to write her memories for this issue of *Sinister Wisdom*. She responded, "…I don't have an article to write, but I did go to the Hamptons to meet Marijane Meaker and we had a wonderful lobster dinner!" This provocative remark led Maida Tilchen to interview Maureen on Zoom on November 11, 2024 to learn the whole story.

Photo Credit: Maureen C.

Maureen met with Marijane Meaker in September 1997. Maureen was forty-two, and Meaker was seventy. Maureen saw an ad for a paperback exposition in New York City, which said that Marijane Meaker would be there to speak and sign books.

Maureen, who has always lived in Ottawa, Canada, says: "I had learned a lot about early lesbian writers over the twenty-five years I had been collecting classic and pulp novels, particularly those that are now known as vintage paperback originals. I had read an article by Barbara Grier in an anthology of writings from *The Ladder*, published by Diana Press in 1976, called *The Lesbians Home Journal*. In it, Grier writes: "1955 saw the first of the noisy nasty titles of the brilliant by deliberately cruel Ann Aldrich...We Walk Alone." She adds that Aldrich is also Vin Packer. I learned more over the years about the feud between Ann Aldrich and The Ladder. So, when I saw Marijane Meaker was featured at a paperback expo, I decided to try to meet her.

I just decided to find her, I'm just that kind of person, I could do it and it worked out much better than I might have expected. She was hospitable. It was lovely." Maureen also mentioned being motivated by a breakup, her mother's recent death, and having some money to spend.

She found Meaker's phone number and address in an online search. Meaker lived in Easthampton. After making sure she could stay with friends in NY, Maureen called her, leaving a message asking to have a meal with her near her home. She still has the tape of Meaker's enthusiastic voicemail response. "I'd never been to the Hamptons before, never thought about going there or that I would know somebody there." Meaker suggested a motel for her to stay in called "Cozy Cabins" with the restaurant right across Montauk Highway.

Maureen didn't think Meaker had been asked about Aldrich or Packer for a long time except to sign books because at the beginning of their first telephone conversation, Meaker asked, "So you don't know who I am now?" Maureen said she didn't. Meaker then explained that she was the award-winning M.E. Kerr, author of young adult novels.

In New York, Maureen rented a car and drove to Easthampton. She remembers it was a few days before the funeral for Princess Diana and the paperback exposition. She describes their meeting as follows, "we had a wonderful lobster dinner! I had a lot of questions and probably talked about myself too much. Lots of laughs, several hours of conversation, and I have a couple of photos of us. We talked briefly about Princess Diana, who Meaker didn't like."

Meaker told Maureen about the 1950s pulp industry and working at Fawcett Gold Medal with editor Dick Carroll, who pushed Fawcett to publish the early pulps. After *We Walk Alone*, subtitled *Through Lesbos' Lonely Groves* and written by Meaker under the pseudonym Ann Aldrich, was published in 1955, Meaker received many letters from readers. She answered one from a woman asking her then what Maureen had asked in 1997: she wanted to meet. "Meaker was as gracious to Ann as she was to me, and also took her around and introduced her. Ann started writing and was published under the pseudonym "Ann Bannon." Ann would stay with her in New York, and they maintained a friendship. "Then something happened, I'm not sure what, but Meaker came away with this idea that Ann had stolen her place as the prominent writer about lesbians in Greenwich Village. She called Ann 'a snake in the grass.' They had some falling out because of it. So, when we were talking, I said to her that it was so long ago and Ann Bannon seems like a lovely person these days, maybe you could get back in touch with her and make amends or patch it up. The next thing I know they were photographed together, and they got to know each other again. There is a photo of them at some book thing together. I found it online with an article which I could not find today. Bannon is quoted as saying, 'we lost touch and I'm really sorry about it.' That article was from twenty years or so back, not a recent quote for an obituary." Maureen notes that almost the only photos on Meaker's Facebook page are of her and Bannon.

Meaker also told Maureen about her relationship with writer Patricia Highsmith. Highsmith had made anti-Semitic remarks during a rare reunion many years after their relationship ended which left Meaker aghast. Maureen thinks she never spoke to her again. Maureen was fascinated and suggested that Meaker write a book about it—and then she did! Meaker's memoir *Highsmith, A Romance of the 1950s* was published in 2003. Their dinner went on for hours, "We drank a bit too much. She took a taxi home. I was staying right across the street. It was just amazing."

"A few days later I went to see her at the book signing. We walked out of it together and we went to a place called the Park Hyatt, I think on Central Park. She used to come into town on the jitney from the Hamptons and use the lobby of that posh hotel as her office, so we sat there and talked a bit more. I brought a whole lot of presents for her—a fridge magnet and a note card of *We Walk Alone*. Also, the videotape of *Forbidden Love: The Unashamed Stories of Lesbian Lives*, which is a 1982 Canadian-made "hybrid drama-documentary" which includes dramatized scenes from Beebo Brinker and other pulp references, plus an interview with Ann Bannon. Meaker had never seen it, so I have a note she sent me about how much she liked the movie. She had no idea people were re-interested in these books. She had gone on to be another type of writer and hadn't come out as the author of the lesbian pulps, except in dribs and drabs. The advertisement for that paperback exposition was maybe the first time she publicly admitted she had written under the names Vin Packer and Ann Aldrich. The ad didn't say "lesbian pulp" at all.

"Afterwards, basically we became friends and corresponded for about eight to ten years, exchanging Christmas cards, notes, and emails. She sent me uncorrected proofs of her new book *Blood on the Forehead* and copies of all of her new books. One was *Deliver Us from Evie*, written under the pseudonym M.E. Kerr, a lesbian adolescent book. I sent her books to sign, and she sent them back. We didn't do much on Facebook, but we were Friended."

Marijane inscribed a copy of Take a Lesbian to Lunch to Maureen but misremembered the month of their lobster dinner.

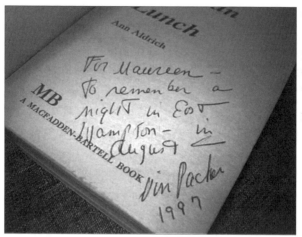

Photo Credit: Maureen C.

What about Meaker's bad reputation? In early issues of *The Ladder*, there were heated letters complaining about what we might now call Meaker's internalized homophobia, prompted by negative portrayals of lesbians in her nonfiction books written under the name Ann Aldrich.

"I know all about it. In her nonfiction book *Carol In a Thousand Cities* (1960), she has a chapter called 'The Ladder, Rung by Rung.' I asked her why. She referenced a Ladder cover of a butch giving a Christmas present to a femme, wrapped messily. I've never seen that cover, but she told me that it just put her off of that *Ladder* issue. I think she didn't relate to butch/femme roles. She didn't want to go into the butch/femme bars in Greenwich Village. I think she felt that *The Ladder* didn't represent her. She was kind and lovely and not at all homophobic at all. I think she felt bad about *The Ladder* thing. I'm sure she regretted it."

(Note: the chapter '"The Ladder, Rung by Rung"' negatively summarizes an entire year of The Ladder, particularly the short stories. Digitized issues of The Ladder can be found online from various sources. For more about Meaker's bad rep, google "Aldrich and The Ladder").

In *Highsmith, a Romance of the 50s*, Meaker discusses asking Highsmith about the title of the anthology she was working on,

Carol in a Thousand Cities. The title was a partial line from the final paragraph of The Price of Salt. This shows she was living and very smitten with Highsmith at the time she put that book together for Gold Medal, including the chapter "The Ladder Rung by Rung."

Maureen believes that Highsmith might have had a hand in the chapter. They were both accomplished writers by then, in 1960, Meaker as a mystery writer under the name Vin Packer, as well as Aldrich. "I can see them writing it together, making fun (drunkenly) of the writing and content of The Ladder. I think it is well known that Grier's mission as the editor of The Ladder then was to get things "out there" no matter the quality. So, the fact that The Ladder was hugely important to the community was less on their minds than their opinion of the quality of the writing.

"There's a book she wrote the foreword to under the pseudonym M.E. Kerr, Hearing Us Out: Voices from the Gay and Lesbian Community (1997), an anthology of teenager's coming out stories. She wrote something I've never seen elsewhere that her parents were very homophobic and so was everybody in her hometown of Auburn, New York. But the main thing she ended with was that her parents missed out on getting to know her and her friends. It was their loss. You can tell by that that she was proud."

Photo Credit: Maureen C.

Maureen C. with Marijane Meaker, September 1997, the Hamptons, NY

MY PASSION FOR PULPS

Ruth Dworin

In 1975, I was a newly-minted baby dyke trying to find my way in the strange new world of Toronto's lesbian-feminist community. As I was always more comfortable with books than people, one of my first stops was the Toronto Women's Bookstore. Along with copies of *Rubyfruit Jungle* and *Patience and Sarah*, *Off Our Backs* and *The Other Woman*, I found a newsprint journal called *Margins*. I was intrigued by an article called "Some Pulp Sappho" by Maida Tilchen (who I later had the privilege of meeting!) and Fran Koski. This article introduced me to the fascinating world of lesbian pulp fiction, and from there the hunt was on! It felt to me that these books were an important part of our "herstory" and needed to be preserved.

In those days, there were plenty of second-hand bookstores with piles and piles of dusty paperbacks. With a good eye and sense of decoding the text of the titles (any title with "strange" "odd" "weird" "girls" or "women" bore closer examination), the pulps were not hard to find. It didn't take me long to amass a small collection. I was helped by Barbara Grier's *The Lesbian in Literature,* particularly the first edition before the (t) (for trash) titles were expunged! I found it particularly ironic that a number of my best finds, including Vin Packer aka Marijane Meaker's *Spring Fire,* were from the Salvation Army book racks – a notoriously homophobic organization! No road trip was complete without a stop at a small-town bookstore, an excellent source of treasures.

I tried to share my "finds" with the Toronto lesbian-feminist community and was surprised at being met with mixed reactions. Some people denounced the books as "politically incorrect" because they perpetuated a butch-femme stereotype which (at that time) we were meant to be escaping. However, I also noticed that when I passed my treasures around at community meetings, some of them did not make it back to me.

Gradually, other women quietly began to gift me with their own books or collections. My first copy of Ann Bannon's *I am a Woman* had masking tape blocking the covers. The woman who gave it to me explained that she had read it on the subway and was terrified that someone would see her reading it so had taped over the covers.

I gradually met other collectors - Maureen Cullingham from Ottawa, who I'd stayed with while attending my first Lesbian Conference, and Robin Cohen from Denver (where I'd grown up) in a car ride after a music festival. We had some lovely visits hunting together, I got to introduce Maureen to Toronto's used bookstore "strips", and Robin and I spent a memorable afternoon digging through someone's basement, sent there by a friend of mine who ran a bookstore in Denver.

Fast forward to 1984. By this point I've been attending and working at womyn's music festivals since 1976 and producing womyn's music concerts in Toronto since 1977. I was overjoyed to receive an invitation from my friend Toni Armstrong Jr. to be Ann Bannon's "artist friend" at the 1984 National Women's Music Festival! This role consisted mainly of making sure she was comfortable in her room, escorting her to workshops and taking her out to dinner. It was an incredible privilege to get to hang out with one of my idols, hear gossip from the 1960's lesbian scene in New York, and have my suspicions confirmed about a few writers from that era. I also got to finally meet Maida Tilchen! Ann was incredibly sweet, generous, and kind, and we corresponded for several years afterwards, she would send me postcards from her travels!

In 1988, my books were invited to become movie stars! My friend Lynne Fernie and her co-director Aerlyn Weissman were starting work on a ground-breaking film, *Forbidden Love: The Unashamed Stories of Lesbian Lives* with the support of Canada's National Film Board (NFB). The film interspersed interviews of lesbians who'd been active in the 50's and 60's with a drama heavily influenced by the pulps. Shots of my covers acted as the bridge between the elements! After a few attempts to shoot the covers in my poorly-lit apartment, I loaned my collection to Lynne and Aerlynn for a few months so they could have easier access for their shots. The books came back in excellent condition, and they gifted me with some additions to my collection! Ann Bannon appeared in the film, and I think I helped connect them with some of their other "stars". The film premiered in 1992 at the Toronto International Film Festival, to great acclaim. It was so exciting to attend the premiere and see my name in the credits!

In 2002, I became a mother on very short notice. I had two weeks to make space in my tiny apartment for an active toddler, and my book collection needed a new home. It went to a friend's basement for a while, and then another friend's garage. Neither were safe environments for these fragile and now extremely hard-to-find books. By this point I think my collection totaled around 500 volumes, mostly pulps but also some hardcover first editions. My treasures included a fairly complete set of pulps written by Marion Zimmer Bradley and Barbara Grier under various pseudonyms for Monarch (you could always tell when an actual lesbian was writing for Monarch, as the book would contain a fairly positive portrayal with the main character either dying or turning straight in the last 3 pages) as well as most of the Fawcett Gold Medal titles written by Marijane Meeker, again under various pseudonyms.

So, I started asking around. By a stroke of sheer luck, my co-worker at Inanna Publications at York University, Vicky Drummond, was friendly with a librarian who worked with the Clara Thomas Archives at York's Scott Library, and they were interested in acquiring my collection. They also got all my papers from my years working in the lesbian-feminist community and producing concerts. It was hard to let them go. I gave them my notes and letters from Ann Bannon to add to the archives, looked at my collection nicely spread out on a series of library tables, and cried.

But I was also comforted to know that the books would be in a safe, climate-controlled environment and would be available to generations yet to come of those who wanted access to these materials. By now, my vision of preserving this slice of our "herstory" was valued by the larger world.

AUNT JULIE AND ME

Robin Cohen

In 1978, at the end of a long day in the kibbutz pickle factory, I used to peruse the shelves of their small hodgepodge library of left-behind donated travelers' books, when one paperback spine jumped out at me. The spine read " I am a Woman". Expecting who knows what kind of anti-feminist tract, I pulled it out. The title was "I am a Woman in Love with a Woman, must society reject me?" by Ann Bannon. I was 21 and felt I was reading my own story at last – that of an isolated young lesbian trying to find her way within a hidden subculture that separated me far from my roots and family. The finding led me to discover other 1950s lesbian pulp fiction, full of the same pathos of our own tortured condemned emotions, secret subculture and stories previously unknown, hidden from history. I found a slew of them while still in Israel. This started me on a lifelong search for more of these books and their hidden authors.

When I came back to the States a year later, the first thing I did was go looking for the mysterious, unknown figure, Ann Bannon. I found her in the most serendipitous, amazing way within a month of my return. I don't think that she was ready to be found yet, but that's a different story, told in my YouTube video memoir, *My Life in the Pulps*.

I found more of the books in funky old bookstores across the West and put together an educational slideshow on them and their importance to our history, shown over the years as an evening's entertainment and at many lesbian and gay events. I called the slideshow "Tripping Over Our Roots." From 1982 through 2000 I did lots of these fun, educational, entertaining evenings, and slideshows on these forgotten beloved lesbian pulps.

From my twenties to my forties, I became a grassroots scholar on the lesbian pulps, this taboo topic unwelcome in academia. I collected hundreds of lesbian pulps over thirty years, rediscovering the real authors, corresponding with them, thanking them for their contributions, and gathering their own stories of how they came to write them. The grassroots popularity of my lesbian pulps slideshows ran through the 1980s and 1990s but eventually waned and I put the slide show aside in about 2001.

Fast forward to August 2005 when Katherine Forrest came out with the paperback anthology, *Lesbian Pulp Fiction* with twenty-two excerpts from the very best of the 1950 to 1965 paperback original lesbian pulps. I picked it up out of casual interest to see which pulps she'd selected. Katherine's personal story, which she shared in her intro, was similar to my own. The pulps were a lifeline to her personal survival, and she held them dear – as an educated lesbian, they were a most valued yet private possession.

Quickly scanning the table of contents, I saw that I was equally familiar with the same authors' true names and backstories. However, there was one author who she deeply thanked in the intro who was unknown to me and previously to Katherine. The ordinary sound in the common name of this unknown author of lesbian pulp fiction sounded off a strange "where have I heard this before" bell in my brain. A week earlier, I had received an unannounced package from my mother, a signed hardback book from a great-aunt whom I'd only met once at age ten when we had visited NYC for the 1964 World's Fair.

I did vaguely know she was a very prolific author of hardback historical fiction and dedicated each of her scores of books to a different set of relatives. It was a very big deal to others in my large, no-college-education extended family to have a writer in the family and a book dedicated to each of them by name! When my mother had found a used copy of one of her books, dedicated to my two brothers and me on her summer in NY flea market jaunts, my mom sent me this book of my aunt's signed to me. I'd opened the unexpected package, seeing that it was a book I, ever the intellectual snob, would never read, and set it aside on my desk without much more thought.

I'd spent the thirty years of my adult life totally divorced from my immediate and extended family. Coming out when I had, in the mid-1970s, we left what we considered the mainstream straight life behind and divorced our families of origin to go "In the Life" as it was called. I was also the only one of my siblings or even first cousins who was a college or university graduate. I lived in the Far West, alienated from my immediate and extended New York family for all of the 1970s, 80s and beyond.

I didn't go to any of the many big life event gatherings of my extended Jewish family, the East Coast bar/bat mitzvahs, the weddings etc. I alone among them lived a very different life, typical of my era of early coming out, a lesbian alone among my siblings and cousins, had no marriage and no children. While living "In The Life" was where I belonged, not having built my own, I longed for family, especially on Jewish or Christian holidays. Even generic old Thanksgiving was a sad, difficult, ever-changing scramble to cadge an invite somewhere. So, I had spent these three decades living the life I'd read in my pulps – as tortured as those in *A World Divided* with my necessarily closeted professional life as an engineer contrasted with my existence as a lesbian activist, educator and entertainer outside my workplace.

With that puzzling, where have I heard this before bell in my brain going off, I looked harder at that aunt-signed book on my desk that I had received the week before. Sure enough, it too was written by Julie Ellis, the exact same pen name Katherine Forrest mentioned as a pulps author new to her. A very common pen name I'm sure I thought, as right away I googled "Julie Ellis author". This pulled up a web-published text interview with a Julie Ellis I had read years before - an author who worked at Midwood, an NYC early 1960s paperbacks only (PBO) publisher. This Julie Ellis who did indeed write all sorts of what she called sleaze 1960s pulps for the early 1960s "male interest" publisher Midwood Tower. I didn't collect Midwood's much because they were mostly awful, so late in the pulp years and written by men for the most part, with only one or two exceptions, complete trash- evident of the slide from 1950s lesbian pulps written by women to early 1960s sleaze. This Julie Ellis said she'd used so many pseudonyms she wasn't even sure she could remember them but said she used some various combinations of her children's names, Susan Richard, Jill Monte etc.

Jill Monte? Well, that lesbian pulp book was one of the 60+ I had on my shelf for thirty years, but it wasn't a Midwood, it was a Domino, a totally respectable mainstream 1960s publisher, so apparently this Midwood sleaze writer Julie Ellis had written that one too. I quickly dug up my two very oldest lesbian lit bibliographies, when they still listed lesbian trashy 1960s pulps, designated with a T for trash, but again nope. No Jill Monte, nor Julie Ellis, only a Joan Ellis (another unrelated common pseudonym).

In those days, when one didn't make long-distance calls without thinking about the cost, I made a quick late call to my friend Ruth, a collector in Canada who gathered sleazier and later stuff including Midwood's, to see if she knew who this Julie Ellis was. We didn't talk long but she didn't know her either.

It was getting very late, but my mind was racing on this. I called my mom right away. I had been out over thirty years and my mom knew I collected lesbian pulps, though it isn't something she liked to think about, certainly not something I would bring up to her. I asked her how her visit with Aunt Julie had been, then tentatively asked if she thought there was any remote possibility our Aunt Julie was writing as early as the early to mid-1960s – and maybe even writing books "like those I collect".

"Absolutely no way", my bleached blond brassy 73-year-old mother rasped. "Those names are just a coincidence, your Aunt Julie is a very successful writer of always well written, very tasteful, good books, and definitely never been gay like you so forget it". She even wore gloves and a hat to their lunch when she signed the book for my mother, my mother added. In a bit of a huff, my mother ended the call, giving me my aunt's phone number and telling me that I needed to call her and thank her for the autographed book.

It was too late to call New York by now, though I did lay awake for quite a while, my mind absolutely racing. The next morning, as soon as the time difference allowed, I called my 86-year-old Aunt whom I'd never spoken to as an adult and shyly introduced myself and thanked her for the gift. She told me that my mother had said I loved to read and that she'd been glad to sign it, hearing I was quite a reader myself. To which I responded, "Yes, I have a great collection of many kinds of books, especially by women authors".

After some more very nervous chatting on my part, I took a deep breath and asked her if she might have written a book called *A World Divided* under the name Jill Monte, a book that I had owned myself for 25 years. In her quavery very sweet old lady voice, she asked me who the publisher was, and I told her Domino. She told me, "Oh yes, a British publisher, why yes I did write a book or two for them, a lesbian story I think? it was?" So, I asked her the bigger question had she ever written for a publisher called Midwood Tower in the 1960s? The answer was why yes, she wrote zillions of books for them, mostly pretty sleazy stuff but that's how she got her start as an author.

So then for the first time, I came out to someone in my extended family. I spilled the story of my books, collecting for over thirty years. Though we few lesbian collectors of the 1980s had figured out numerous pseudonyms —Ann Bannon who I corresponded with in the early 1980s after her rediscovery, Patricia Highsmith the suspense author, Marion Zimmer Bradley the science fiction author, none of us ever deciphered all the lost pulps authors, including whoever was the real author behind Joan Ellis who wrote *The Third Street, Gay Girl, In the Shadows, Forbidden Sex,* and *Campus Kittens* among other Midwood's.

She told me no one else in the family beyond her own children had known of the Midwood sleaze books that launched her writing career later into gothics and then eventually family sagas. She told me she had written a book a week for Midwood. She said she was so popular and successful that despite the times, lesbian groups would write to her to ask her when her next book was coming out. She also explained that she insisted her lesbian stories always have a happy ending despite what the men in charge at Midwood wanted and despite the understandable fears of her two lesbian Midwood colleagues.

So yes indeed, I'd been collecting, grassroots researching, and educating on the lesbian pulps for thirty years, and I just figured out that my own Aunt wrote sympathetic lesbian pulps, including one that had been on my shelf for more than twenty-five years.

As we spoke more, she explained that because of Katherine Forrest's new lesbian pulp fiction anthology, she had been invited to do a panel with two other still-living lesbian pulp writers at the New York City gay literature club. Would I like to come?

Would I? You bet I went!

Ill health and cancellations by the other two elderly New York area lesbian pulp authors (Marijane Meaker and Sally Singer – March Hastings in Midwood days) canceled the once-in-a-lifetime panel soon after I bought my plane ticket, but I had a fantastic visit with my very sweet and very liberal 86-year-old Aunt, who welcomed me as a large, connected family always does.

While visiting with her, I also learned that she and another lesbian pulp author had been the featured authors at the 2003 Paperback convention in NYC, and these two gentle elderly grandmotherly types had become friends – my aunt and Ann Bannon! It was through Ann, now called Queen of the Pulps, that Katherine found my aunt.

My aunt recounted how at the convention she had been mobbed by collectors of her scores and scores of sleaze titles, all seeking her valued signature on the trashy paperbacks she'd written that launched her successful very long and prolific paperback then hardback family sagas career.

I felt like at last my life had come full circle. The separate, "In The Life" part of me, now joined with the family parts for the first time – for the first time I felt I was not living in "a world divided".

Aunt Julie told me she'd also written and produced a lesbian play in 1959 in Greenwich Village though she'd had a hard time finding actresses willing to appear in it at the time and now that Katherine was appreciating her lesbian writing she was combing her file of manuscripts for that 1959 lesbian play.

She had fought her Midwood publishers to insist on happy lesbian endings when no one would, including the lesbians who wrote there but couldn't advocate for themselves. When our stories were required to end with suicides, last-minute recants or marriages on the final page of the book, her stories ended with the women happily together because she insisted on it.

And where exactly was that play? She was looking all over for it now – in her good-sized NYC apartment, literally overflowing with shelves of her own published Julie Ellis hardbacks. She couldn't find it but was going to keep looking.

On my Facebook page, where it is seen by my wonderful accepting senior adult cousins whose weddings were long ago avoided but whose children's bar mitzvahs and weddings I've attended, is a picture that was sent to me by Ann Bannon, aka the queen of the lesbian pulps, viewable on her website AnnBannon.com labeled "me and author Julie Ellis". There's Ann Bannon and my little 4-foot-something tall 84-year-old Aunt a head shorter in a grand hat, the two women grinning together. Aunt Julie died in her sleep at home of an overnight stroke just three months after our visit. She had three unfinished books that she was in the middle of writing and never did find that 1959 lesbian play she'd written and produced in Greenwich Village.

I revived the slide show, changed the ending, and made a YouTube video called *My Life in the Pulps* about my more than forty years of lesbian pulps collecting and author encounters; it ends with the song Imagine My Surprise and a dedication to Julie Ellis: real name Marilyn Wasserman. Instead of ending as the show did, with a quote about finding and saving our lost stories, the video ends with a photo of my tiny little Aunt and me, with me holding up all her lesbian pulps and the 2005 Lesbian Pulps anthology book in our hands, laughing together in front of her crammed bookcases.

ORAL HISTORY

"WE WERE NOT A WOMEN'S BOOKSTORE, WE WERE A FEMINIST BOOKSTORE": FROM AN ORAL HISTORY OF LINDA BRYANT

Dartricia Rollins

This oral history was conducted on January 31, 2023, in Linda Bryant's home as part of Charis' digital campaign, "You Had to Be There." This excerpt has been edited for clarity.

Linda Bryant was born in 1948 in Paducah, Kentucky. She moved to Atlanta in 1970 and co-founded Charis Books and More in 1974 with Barbara Borgman. Linda now lives in Decatur, Georgia with her wife Wendy E. Belkin. This excerpt begins with Linda Bryant, the co-founder of Charis Books, speaking about her relationship with the Atlanta Lesbian Feminist Alliance who were founded around the same time as Charis Books and More. Linda discusses coming out, being in a relationship with Kay Hagan, women's music history, attending Women in Print for the first time, and identifying as a feminist bookstore. Later in the conversation, she discusses programs at Charis Books and More, the founding of Charis Circle, and some of the important people in the bookstore's history that shaped it into what would become the store's future.

Linda Bryant: I did not come out until 1978. They [Atlanta Lesbian Feminist Alliance] were all so happy when I got there. I just got there by falling in love, which is kind of how I do everything. So they were friends and supporters of Charis. The women's music started up, you know, about that same time. And Chris Carol was a distributor for music. And so she would come in the store. It was the early women's music era, we're talking about Cris Williamson, and Meg Christian, and Kay Gardner. And I don't know if you know, that little piece about Swallow Hollow, and Kay Gardner. But Marilyn [Ries], who was Sorrel's [Hays] partner, was a sound engineer and she helped to produce Kay Gardner's first album, which was called Moon Circles, beautiful flute music. So we would play music in the store all the time. We had a record player I believe or it could have been a cassette player, but I think it was a record player. We played those things and fell in love with them. I mean, everybody fell in love with Cris Williamson's, "The Changer and the Changed." It was just such an iconic thing. It played all the time and people loved it. I remember going to hear Cris Williamson at some bar or something before I came out, you know, just because she was cool. And I liked her. So we got to know some of the ALFA people through that, too. And Eleanor Smith is another really important person in that I think she wrote the first article about Charis in the ALFA newsletter. I was never very involved with ALFA. And one of the reasons was because I was a single parent. I was busy. I was very busy. I became a parent before I came out. And I was very good friends with a lot of the people who were in ALFA. And I felt they were very much a part of Charis but it was not like a personally pivotal thing for me.

Dartricia Rollins: Tell me about when Charis then came to identify as a feminist bookstore.

Linda Bryant: Well, we didn't know that there were feminist bookstores. We didn't know anything about that. In 1981 we went to Women in Print, which was a pivotal moment in the life of Charis. Sandra [Gail Lambert], Kay Hagan, and I drove to the DC area, and stayed in a dorm kind of place. I remember that we were in bunk beds because Kay and I were sweethearts, and you know, we were trying to make do with those bunk beds. But that was a really significant time in the life of feminist bookstores. New Words, and Old Wives Tales, already identified themselves as feminist bookstores, at the time we didn't know they even existed.

I can't say exactly when we said, oh, we're a feminist bookstore, but it was the late 70s, early 80s when we realized that's what we've been doing. That's who we are. And then to be able to read about what other places were doing how they were serving the community and how we could share resources and find out about cool little things to carry once Feminist Bookstore News got started. We were able to help each other out. But Women in Print was not just the bookstores, it was the presses. And that's when so many of the presses were just getting started. We were we were terribly taken with Persephone Press. Persephone Press did *The Coming Out Stories*, *This Bridge*, *Nice Jewish Girls*, and other really great things. Kay and I particularly just fell in love with the women who ran Persephone Press. I remember when they came to town for, Women in Print, or something, and I remember Kay and I buying them this big bouquet of peonies, because they were so beautiful. And we just loved them so much. I don't know, whatever even happened to those women. Persephone got absorbed by something else later. But Women in Print was where they introduced Kitchen Table [Press]. We got to know and have a relationship with Barbara Smith and various people in that world. It was just an amazing time for us. We got to learn about all the issues. No, not all the issues because we were not aware of trans issues at all, at that time. But many of the issues that matter to us and matter to us still were things that were just popping up at Women in Print. Women in Print was very challenging, exciting, and wonderful. And helped to shape Charis I think. I'd say *Feminist Bookstore News* and having that network, that community across the country.

Linda Bryant: Sometime later in our history, Kay and I also went to the [Fifth] International Feminist Book Fair in Amsterdam, which was a great time. That was probably '91 or something. So yeah, feminist bookstores, it was so exciting to be able to name it. And we were always very clear that we were not a women's bookstore, we were a feminist bookstore. Because we were never exclusively for women, even in the most separatist days, when that didn't necessarily go over big with some of our separatist sisters. We did have a few women-only events such an event for *Lesbian Sex* for Joanne Loulan when that book came out, or you know, a few things like that, but, when we did do those things, we faced a lot of conversation about that. Which for us preceded any awareness of trans issues.

Another example is that we always knew that men mattered. Barbara was married to a man and she stayed with us for five years and remains my precious dear friend to this day, I mean, I was dating men, but the holistic vision that came out of our Christian roots was always about everyone. It was always about a world that could live in harmony and justice, peace, and love.

We got involved in the early days of the peace movement, we held events, and went to a peace encampment at the Savannah River Plant, in probably 1979. Sandra Lambert also participated in the peace walk from Gainesville, Florida to Key West. And Barbara Deming was in Key West and lived there in community with other women. And so this was a peace walk. And so people would join for just periods. I went down for a week or something like that, and did fifteen miles a day, and just talked to people and camped out or stayed in churches or whatever, and just wanted to stand for peace. That was never just a women's-only movement.

Dartricia Rollins: Tell me about the culture or how you all created programming around that time that started to have like a more feminist lens or just tell me about Charis programming in general.

Linda Bryant: Well, I know that when we became Charis Circle, we had been doing weekly programming for eighteen years already. Because when we wrote our proposal to become a 501(c)3, we had flyers from eighteen years of programs. At least, that's my memory, and I think that's accurate. We had various people involved at different times in our history, but I recall Sandra, Sherry, and Maya being very important in the development of programs. We were always so busy, but we cared about what was going on in the world. I was particularly busy as a single parent and didn't have the time to go to meetings to find venues to host programs. So we just decided to have them at the bookstore. And that's kind of how programming developed.

Somebody would come to town and we would want to hear what they had to say and we created a space where we could do that. In the beginning, we didn't have everything on wheels. We eventually put all bookshelves on wheels, so we could move things around. Eventually, somebody donated these little wooden chairs to us that we kept in the basement, which belonged to Abba Dabba. It was called the wizard's cellar, there was a little spot down there, and they provided us with a space to store our chairs.

Sherry Emery was very instrumental in getting the volunteers set up because she had really strong relationships with people. And again, I had a little kid at home. And so I didn't do all the programs. But Sherry did. And Sherry had her little core volunteers who came and rotated on Thursday nights. They would come and go to the basement and get the chairs, set the chairs up, and we would have a program. So that just kind of evolved. At first, we would maybe just have a reading, you have someone like Kay Hagan and Pearl Cleage do poetry readings, probably 1981-ish. Then other people would come to do readings or they just needed a little space for something. It was such a tiny space that we would sometimes have to squeeze in and stand. It took a while to evolve into what it became when Maya came to work with us.

The space on the corner became available, and she put some money in and we broke down the walls between the two spaces, then we had more room to be able to have a program and have the chairs all set up. So I think the chairs didn't come in until after Maya was there. *laughter* Because you had to have space to put them. I don't think we had those chairs before that. Once we had that corner space, we could do more. Even in the very beginning, we had more room for people to just sit on the floor and have a children's story hour or something. We were just trying to figure out what we were doing.

Dartricia Rollins: Who were some of the people who would come and do readings? Do you have a, I'm sure there are no favorites, but do you have any stories?

Linda Bryant: Well, Nikky Finney came early on, how old was she? She must have been so young. And I can just see her standing by the steps going into the loft. Big ol', you know, what Nikky looks like tall and regal and gorgeous. She was so young then. And so I remember that. And Shay [Youngblood] always loves to tell the story of herself doing her first reading there, and how that came about. And how shocked she was when I said well, then you should come do a reading because she told me she was a writer. Okay, you should come do a reading. And so some of those kinds of things happened. Sometimes it was somebody who sang, like Jan Gibson, who was the singer for Moral Hazard, Jan was incredibly talented, and amazing, and it was wonderful to have her there. Elise Witt, coming and singing, as Elise Witt and the Small Family Orchestra, is what they were then. And so she and her sister Mary, coming and singing in those first 10 years, I would say. And then you know programs kind of grew out of all of that.

Linda Bryant's oral history was conducted as part of Charis Books and More/Charis Circle's 2023 digital women's history month campaign, "You Had to Be There." The campaign included documents and photographs from Charis' archive spanning from 1974-2023. The final audio and transcripts will be available and archived as part of the Charis Books and More/Charis Circle collection at the Sallie Bingham Center for Women's History and Culture at Duke University.

ART ESSAYS

PERENNIALS: LESBIAN FEMINISM AND NARRATIVES OF LIBERATION IN THE ART OF SAMANTHA NYE

Cassandra Langer

In "Narratives of Liberation: Pluralities of Hope," lesbian feminist writer Joan Nestle declares, "Our narratives of liberation begin with a touch, begin with a body, asking for pleasure that has no such social place."[1] Thanks to multidisciplinary artist Samantha Nye's imagination, we have depictions of those social spaces.

Nye is a lesbian feminist and a native of Hollywood, Florida. She attributes her inclination to performance art to her relatively brief appearances as a "perfect" Gerber baby and child model. Her early encounters with a performative self and identity have shaped her studio practices in paintings, videos, and installation by reimagining a space of "seduction through reenactment," an area that many find titillating or frightening.

Fabulism, magic realism, and the creation of images depicting this social space through a lesbian sensibility are the stuff of Samantha Nye's art. Her video installations include "My Heart's in a Whirl" (2021), a project that remakes the Scopitone classics and short musical films that preceded MTV and YouTube. Nye's most recent video performance, "Daddy" (2018), is one of the most unruly, vulgar, savage, and outright hilarious satires by a contemporary feminist lesbian artist I have ever seen. In this campy, sexually charged romp, the artist's mother stars as a woman seeking a "daddy" by auditioning five different butches to demonstrate their skills. In a bait and switch, Nye stands in for her mother, snatching the sexual benefits offered for herself using a cornucopia of sex toys.

---

1 Joan Nestle, "Narratives of Liberation: Pluralities of Hope," in *A Sturdy Yes of a People: Selected Writings* (Dover, Florida: Sinister Wisdom, 2022).

As for her paintings, Nye restages photographer Slim Aarons' "Attractive People Doing Attractive Things in Attractive Places," a series of seventies glamorous poolside photographs reimagined as reflections of her sapphic revisions. Aarons' work features groups of wealthy celebrities and socialites lounging in luxurious tropical settings. In Nye's painting, she inserts lesbian and trans couples in a series of cutting-edge riffs on straight pool parties, ski resorts, and tropical villas.

Before launching into a full-blown discussion of Nye's defining visual narratives on gender, sexuality, and aging, let me set the stage for the feminist liberation during the seventies as well as my lesbian art criticism. Feminist critics as varied as Kate Millett, Cindy Nemser, and Lucy Lippard challenged the art establishment. For example, they showed how phallic criticism typecasts women according to clichés associated with female biology, and in turn, they completely rethought how they practiced art criticism—their work initiated new directions for both writing criticism and making art. In addition, artists Judy Chicago and Mimi Shapiro, as well as art historian Patricia Minardi, believed that men's and women's different social and biological experiences offered clues to women's different sensibilities.

It has been more than forty-five years since feminists initiated this pioneering work. Second-wave female artists used traditional and avant-garde media to focus on subject matter, content, and materials (i.e., fabric, fiber, and clay) that the white male art establishment ignored and avoided.

Hannah Wilke, Carolee Schneemann, and Joan Semmel used their creativity to depict sexuality, aesthetic pleasure, and power for women. May Stevens, Judy Chicago, and Mimi Shapiro put political and social consciences into their work against war and patriarchy. Mary Beth Adelson, Ana Mendieta, and Betye Saar explored the love and power associated with the Great Goddess archetype.

Lesbian artists, including Harmony Hammond, Joan E. Biren (JEB), Tee Corinne, Janet Cooling, Hollis Sigler, Louise Fishman, Deborah Kass, Patricia Cronin, Nancy Fried, and Christina Schlesinger pushed heterosexist limits beyond the margins by depicting the lesbian body in new and exciting ways.

Following the leads of Lippard and Nemser, feminist art critics, including myself, Arlene Raven, and Joanna Frueh further defined a working model of American feminist art criticism. Some established art historians insisted that we were an outlaw breed despite the groundbreaking work of female art historians Eleanor Tufts, Linda Nochlin, and Ann Harris that crossed existing distinctions between art history and art criticism. My work focuses on three points: deconstructing patriarchal art history, constructing a lesbian gaze, and modeling lesbian feminist art criticism seen through a gynocentric and prismatic lens.

Photo Credit: Samantha Nye

"Daddy," 2018

The Armory Show and Samantha Nye

Since its inception in 1913, the Armory Show has been controversial. Widely advertised, the New York Art Fair is an international art extravaganza that rivals the Metropolitan Museum of Art's Costume Institute red carpet fundraiser (the Met Gala). The Armory Show attracts its share of poseurs, con artists, social climbers, and dedicated art collectors. A VIP invitational precedes the general fair before opening up to the public. Lasting four days, the show hosts a crowd of over 65,000 annually.

This year, the Armory Show consisted of 212 exhibitors from 37 countries—157 in-person exhibitors and 55 virtual exhibitors. The show is a cash cow for dealers, advertisers, and others. For me and other art lovers and critics, it is an opportunity to see what's new and hot in the marketplace, meet up with old friends, enjoy the hype, and meet contemporary artists with something interesting to offer.

At the show, I intended to see art by an interesting lesbian artist whose work I had been introduced to at Candice Madey Gallery in New York. Her name was Samantha Nye, and she originally hailed from South Florida, where I had grown up and come out. When I finally located the Madey booth, I was gobsmacked by the shocked voice of a middle-aged, impeccably designer-dressed, platinum blond in Manolo Blahnik stilettos gasping to her male escort in heavily accented English, "Oh my God, what is that!" Her gaze was riveted on one of Nye's meticulously detailed magic realist visions of mixed-race older women with naked breasts and vaginas bared, sunning themselves and playing cards poolside. I was intrigued by the combination of pagan, earthy, spiritual, and transcendent same-sex joy she created.

Photo Credit: Samantha Nye

Attractive People Doing Attractive Things in Attractive Places

My companion, a culture writer and psychotherapist, turned and whispered to me smiling, "Has she never seen a full-frontal nude before?" I could hardly keep from cracking up at the woman's shock. Across from where we were standing, I could see Samantha talking with two beautiful tattooed young women in leather, lace, and chain necklaces. We introduced ourselves. I mentioned that I had seen her work a week earlier and wanted to interview her. I said that her work reminded me of the lesbian life I had come out into during the sixties.

Interview with Samantha Nye

CL: Can you tell us about your family background?

SAM: I am a South Floridan, born and raised, and I think it shows in my work. My dad lived in Hollywood, Florida his whole life, while my mom was born in St. Louis and made her way to Florida after finishing school. Both sides of my family were Jewish in a cultural but secular way. My mom raised me like a "hippie with a touch of Jewish mysticism." I grew up extremely close to both sides of my grandparents, so I also have Canadian, New York, and Midwest cultural influences.

CL: When did you decide to be an artist, and what is your training?

SAM: I was one of those kids that would spend entire days painting or drawing. My parents really encouraged and valued my interest in art. The theme of my third birthday was painting. It was then that they started calling me an artist, and I just believed them. Nobody in my life was a professional artist, so I never thought about it that way, but every adult in my life had an artistic outlet of some sort. Out of high school, I went directly into a massage therapy program and figured I would paint or draw on the weekends. I never considered college of any kind because there was no money for that endeavor. But in my early twenties, I had a girlfriend who attended a music college, and after visiting her, I suddenly felt certain that I had to study art in a formal way. So, I moved to Northampton, Massachusetts, and enrolled in a community college with the purpose of studying art. Thankfully, my massage practice could pay for those two years, and I got a scholarship to go to The School of the Museum of Fine Arts in Boston where I completed my undergraduate art education.

CL: Samantha, I have to confess. For me, seeing art depicting naked, aging female bodies that are at the same time protected in tropical settings is so special because I grew up in Dade County, came out around 1959–1960, and my lesbian social life was very much like the one reflected in your art. Indeed, it's one thing you don't expect to see at an international art fair. Can you tell us about how you came to create these images?

SAM: I am incredibly honored that my work found its way to you and vice versa. I remember meeting you and hearing your connection to these Miami memories while standing in the Armory booth, and I was just covered in chills. While I was an undergrad, my grandmother and mother were my main subjects for paintings and videos. Then, I expanded to making work with their group of friends, and things started to click for me. I was just so interested in making images with them and truly never entertained working with my aged peers again. I was working on a series of paintings called "Entertainment For Men," which asked these women to pose as Playboy models. I started imagining a related scene where all these women would pose together in the Playboy Pool Grotto. As that idea grew in my mind, I decided to instead look at a reference that was actually very present in mine and the life of these women, which ended up being the poolside photographs of Slim Aarons. I immediately decided that I would not only be including the matriarchs of my family but that I would make this work a queer utopic setting for lesbians over sixty.

CL: I really find it strange how "funny girls" of the sixties and beyond still shock our heterosexists' patriarchally dominated society and culture. I am a film critic and film noir fan, so I am familiar with how the Hollywood sexist wet dream machine has conditioned audiences. Your video takes its name from Laura Mulvey's groundbreaking essay "Visual Pleasure and Narrative Cinema" in which you reenact the musical Scopitone films of the sixties. You camp these with a cast of women ages fifty-five through ninety-two, including your mother, grandmother, their lifelong friends, and elders of the queer community. Your frame-by-frame remakes focus on this cast of elders as objects of my desire or vice versa and envision campy fantasy histories of age, race, disability, and trans-inclusive lesbian spaces.

Photo Credit: Suppressed Histories Archives

Sheela-na-gig from Chloran, Ireland

SAM: I have so many moments from my shows that support this. I have seen several parents dramatically pull their children away from my work and similarly seen straight men reject the path closest to my work as if walking near it would infect them. My wonderful and hilarious curator at the Museum of Fine Arts, Boston, even put up a sign in response to these types of reactions. It said, "The video artwork within this gallery explores the sexuality and eroticism of women and nonbinary people. These are common themes in art history, although we hope if you spend time with the work, you will also understand how this artwork is radically different."

CL: Currently, the small screen streams various lesbian content for general audiences who enjoy these programs on Apple, Netflix, and Hulu. These capitalize on intimate relationships among girls and women (i.e., Netflix's *Wednesday* or Apple's *The Morning*

Show and *Invasion*). Do you think this trend bodes well for young women today, or is it just more of the same titillation for a straight audience?

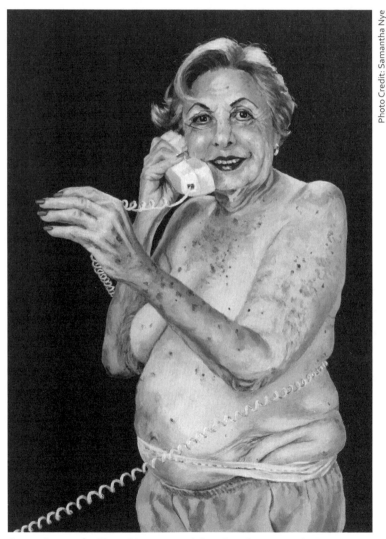

Photo Credit: Samantha Nye

Entertainment for Men – Mommon as July 1982, oil on paper, 8.5" x 11", 2012

SAM: When I was younger, we only had lesbian representation that was aimed at men, and it was still powerful for me in lots of ways. So, I think it's great that there is so much more. I don't necessarily watch much of it, but I believe my students do, and I think it's important for them!

CL: I have to say, as an aging body myself, I never expected to see a woman of your generation interested in painting older women, or, as I like to describe myself and my generation, "elders of the tribe," depicted in all the fullness of life what their bodies, minds, and spirits have experienced: the toll of living in a sexist, racist, white-dominant patriarchal society and culture. The culture we live in has little or no use for women once they are postmenopausal. The only positive lesbian image I've seen recently is the film *Nyad*, starring Annette Bening and Jodie Foster, both in their sixties. I'd like to know more about why you think it's important to depict the realities vital to older women enjoying their aging bodies despite a male-dominated society's need to condition them to denigrate themselves rather than celebrate their lives.

SAM: Well, for one, it's the subject matter that I most want to see AND one I don't see addressed enough. As a younger artist, I was so taken with Barbara Hammer's work, particularly *Dyketactics*, and I started to wonder: where are all those women now? I learned from my grandmother's and mother's communities how vital and strong passion, pleasure, and desire remain even when media and culture tell us they should fade. I didn't realize how much I bought into this idea that women lose their power as they age. In high school, I remember my grandmother asked me to go lingerie shopping with her for a weekend trip with a new boyfriend. I was surprised and then immediately disappointed in my surprise. Once I came out, I was introduced to so many intergenerational dyke communities. And again, I was amazed and surprised at how integral it was in lesbian circles to learn from and value intergenerational relationships. So, my work is a reflection, a thank you, a love letter to those I have learned from. And it is also a "pretty please" for a fun and sexy future.

Photo Credit: Samantha Nye

Statue with bare breasted woman

CL: At the end of the day, where do you see yourself going from here? Is this a passing phase for you?

SAM: I work on a series for a very, very long time. So, I intend to keep this series going for a while. There is just so much more I want to see happen in the work and in these Slim Aarons poolscapes. Technically, it takes a long time to make these paintings, so I don't get to move through ideas as fast as many other painters I know and love. So yes, expect to see many more poolsides dedicated to lesbian utopic scenes. Plus, I am building my perfect future in this work. And that takes a while.

Why Nye's Art Matters

After nearly sixty years as a practicing lesbian feminist art historian and critic, I know that the most challenging part of testing the art establishment's choppy waters is constructing a world without men. It's a risky business and still seen as revolutionary. It means spending time dealing with uncertainties and having the confidence to look, see, and think about creativity and meaning in art and life. I was naturally drawn to Samantha Nye's art because it hit me where I and hundreds of queer women live. The world she created was as natural to me as seeing the trajectory between the feminine world of Marie Laurencin's (1883-1956) imagination that placed women at the center of her art and the world of female agency Nye's art imagines: what a sapphic world without patriarchy could be if we were to live in it right now.

Photo Credit: Marie Laurencin, Centre Pompidou – Musée National d'Art Moderne / Centre de Création Industrielle, Paris. Gift of Lord Joseph Duveen, 1931, on deposit to Musée des Arts Décoratifs, Paris. Artwork © 2023 Fondation Foujita / Artists Rights Society (ARS), New York / ADAGP, Paris. Photo: Jacques Faujour / Digital Image © 2023 CNAC/MNAM, Dist. RMN-Grand Palais / Art Resource, NY

Women with Dove, 1919

By moving into uncharted territory and exploring the body as a site of confrontation, Nye challenges the whole man-made world's sacred cows. In doing so, she exposes herself and her art to the political, social, and aesthetic judgments of a heterosexist, misogynistic, and patriarchal worldview while at the same time presenting a world apart from their universe, thus critiquing its history, values, and morals. Due to her actions, Nye faces some daunting challenges, including dealing with the isolation and marginalization within the women's movement in general, the LGBTQIA2S+ movement, and other social movements, as some may not be recognized or respected for either her art or perspectives. Moreover, she is a mid-career artist juggling her personal and political life while struggling to balance her relationships, values, and goals with others who may not share or support them. Undoubtedly, there will be conflicts and tensions among different groups of lesbians and feminists, as they have different opinions and approaches to achieving their shared vision of liberation. Some will undoubtedly view her visions of lesbian social spaces as politically incorrect and retrograde instead of recognizing them for the revolutionary portrayals that they are. Her art is a love letter to freedom regardless of the controversies accompanying revolutionary concepts.

THROUGH HANDS, STOMACH, AND ROOTS[1]

Fisun Yalçınkaya

In their wallpaper series (dated between 2001 and 2024), artist Şafak Şule Kemancı **(lives and works in Istanbul)** observes intimate scenes among friends and lovers, and celebrates their gestures of love. By transforming these moments into repeating patterns on the wallpapers, they evolve them into shapes of plants. Patterns find their way into roots, foliage, and plant stems and create the hope of building a world of our own. Şafak's wall paper series celebrates queer love and friendship and attempts to open up new ways of thinking about love.

The artist started making these wallpapers years ago in England, where people could express pride about how they could tolerate queers simply by saying so. These series of works were a rebellion against this "toleration" manifested in the sentence "Do what you do in between the four walls of the home." Therefore, the artist simply covered the walls with love and sex. Over the years, **Şafak** continued making these series, and as the bodies and acts of sex in the wallpapers grew and changed, they turned their gaze to the targeted audience of those who are queers and lesbians. The story started with rebellion and now focuses on how we see love and sex. Doesn't give a damn for the rest.[2]

---

1 In one of his poems, İlker Hepkan advises, "Don't leave this life without experiencing deep love with a couple in their bed." His feeling is echoed in the book "Beyefendiler" (Gentlemen), which celebrates queer love, including polyamory, obsessions, and the intricacies of relationships. This collection invites reflection on how love creates new worlds that are difficult to dismantle once formed. It also prompts consideration of those who lack love, contrasting sharply with the romantic notions found in his poetry. This poem was the first thing on my mind when I started thinking about this article. But the title of the article comes from another poem I love, Orhan Veli says in his Dalgacı Mahmut poem, "I have a head in my head / a stomach at my stomach / a foot at my foot / I couldn't know what to do with them". These artists I choose simply knows what to do with their heads / hands, stomachs and foot or roots. Also looking for an answer on not knowing.

2 From the conversation with the artist, dated 9 April, 2024.

Şafak Şule Kemancı Esra and Özge 2021
Digital print wall paper

When I explore these themes of love, life, and the absence of freedom of love, I think of social theories and the performative methodology. I'm interested in understanding why we need aesthetic connections. We gather around similar desires: to live and to express. Is there a bond between life, aesthetics, and art? How are these bonds formed? How do we build and protect our lives through activism and a love of aesthetic expression? What are the visual and audio-tactile shapes of a bond, a relationship? Art provides a lens through which we can examine these questions, and works by queer artists Yaz Taşçı, Okyanus Çağrı Çamcı, and Şafak Şule Kemancı delve deeply into these themes.

All three artists work with their own hands, among other techniques. The power of the painting is coming back in the big art. Artists are exploring old techniques anew. All these artists open a window to the past with performative, experimental methods and materials. To understand these artists and their work, I begin with three examples of the placement of handmade art today. I'll explore the place of painting and "the art made with the artist's own hands" rather than more digitized techniques in the international art scene. Then I turn to the Turkey's art scene to understand these three artists' aims. Finally, through these three artists' works, I explore the past, present, and future as symbolized by roots, stomachs, and hands. I ask: can we find a note or a shape of the queer aesthetic of Istanbul? Finally, I explore why the urge to live and the urge to express it aesthetically come from the same place.

New and Old Places of Painting

Following the 59th and 60th Venice Biennale International Art Exhibition and Documenta Fifteen in Kassel, Germany, in 2022, there has been a significant change in how big institutions define art history and interpret painting. For the 59th Venice Biennale International Art Exhibition, Italian curator Cecilia Alemani was inspired by surrealist painter and writer Leonora Carrington's paintings and her book titled "The Milk of Dreams." Carrington creates a world where anything and anybody can transform into anything they like. This exhibition hosted the works of 200 artists, over 180 of whose works were seen in the biennale for the first time. For the first time in its 127-year history, the Biennale featured a majority of women and gender non-conforming artists. This choice changed the global art landscape shifting away from the male-centric, cis narrative. Alemani's curatorial vision resulted in a proliferation of paintings in the selection, much of which had never before been at the main exhibition of the Biennale and a wider audience for Carrington's paintings. At the Biennale, I felt the most powerful female energy (whatever that is, I still cannot find the words to define it) with the strong aesthetic statements made in the exhibition areas of Arsenale and Giardini during the biennale.

In the same year, Documenta Fifteen held one of the world's largest and most contentious art exhibitions. Documenta, an exhibition organized every five years, commands global attention. For the first time in its history, the Documenta jury assigned curation to a collective from Indonesia called ruangrupa. What they brought to Documenta resulted surprisingly in a worldwide debate about a single painting's influence. A mural by Taring Padi, a collective of undergound artists in Indonesia, titled "Besok Kita (Today they've come for them, tomorrow they come for us)" **(2021),** measuring 8x5 meters was the focus of the debate. "Besok Kita" includes multiple figures; one is an Israeli soldier who looked like a pig. This figure sparked debate about anti-Semitism and freedom of speech. Ultimate the mural was removed from the exhibition, and the controversy prompted the resignation of Sabine Schormann, director-general of Documenta. Documenta Fifteen featured diverse thematic landscapes and presented concepts like "lumbung," "ekosistem," "common pot," "fridskul," and "harvest." The resurgence of painting as a method was overshadowed by the controversy around the one mural.

The power of the art of painting is also evident in last year's 60th Venice Biennale International Art Exhibition (continuing until November 24, 2024). The curator is Adriano Pedrosa, the first South American curator of the Venice Biennale. For the last ten years, he has been the artistic director of the Museum of Art of São Paulo (MASP). He also previously curated the 12th Istanbul Biennial (2011) with Jens Hoffmann. Pedrosa chose the title "Foreigners Everywhere." In the exhibition, he made an architectural choice to underline the experience of displacement and estrangement. Architect Lina Bo Bardi made units from glass, wood, and concrete to hang the paintings not on the walls, but dangling from the ceiling, exposing both the front and back of the paintings. Originally showcased at MASP, these units were relocated to the 60th Venice Biennale International Art Exhibition, highlighting a narrative centered around the painting. With this intervention,

Pedrosa highlighted the notion that we can all potentially become refugees, feeling like strangers; we're all just a little bit far away from losing our surroundings, he stated simply by showing there are two sides of everything. Through the Biennale, he underlines the historical reality that even Europeans, who have long been at the center, were once immigrants themselves.

These examples show that the painting still challenges gender policies, provokes discussions all around the Western art world, and provides a unique aesthetic point of view that can challenge the perspective of the world we live in. These events are quite in the center; they were big, enormous art events that were led by the traditional institutions of the Western art world.

The role of painting and aesthetics are also challenged in different places. Let's turn our gaze to the city where I'm deeply connected with a powerful bond as an art writer and an editor for 15 years now: Istanbul.

Istanbul's Art Scene

Traditional arts in the Ottoman Empire evolved within the constraints of Islamic rules prohibiting figure and portrait drawing to prevent idolatry. They were quite rich in terms of aesthetic representation, but because of Islamic rules, Western painting arrived relatively late to the Ottoman Empire, and when it arrived, the aim of the paintings was simply to document geographical landscapes. Painting began in Turkey with a group called Soldier Painters during the Reorganization (Tanzimat) era in the 19th century. With the establishment of the Republic (1923), building national art became desireable. During the 1950s, talented artists were sent to Paris to study art, where they were exposed to influential art movements such as cubism and impressionism, and when they came back to the motherland, they endeavored to integrate it into Anatolian tradition. Later, the next generation tried to combine the traditional arts of the Ottoman Era with modern techniques.

During and after the 1970s, Istanbul created its own art scene. In 1976, with the opening of the Maçka Art Gallery, a small but quite effective hub for conceptual art and abstract art emerged. They gallery became a place to gather and have discussions on art and architecture, differences and similarities between painting and sculpture, and a meeting point to build different artistic discourses. Founded by two sisters, Rabia Çapa and Varlık Sadıkoğlu, this 80-square-meter gallery, located in a posh neighborhood called Nişantaşı, opened the first solo exhibitions for the artists who would be cherished in the future by the international art world, such as Füsun Onur and Sarkis. Also, new artists emerged through the "Youth Action" series and the "Performance Days" (1996–1997), a platform designed to host art events open to everyone and without a jury. During the 1990s, the impact of Istanbul Biennial, organized by the Istanbul Foundation for Culture and Arts (İKSV), a cornerstone of Istanbul's cultural landscape, since 1987, continued to grow.

The feminist effect in Turkey's art scene started during the 1980s with Nil Yalter's focus on women, migration, and representations of national identity, İpek Duben's interest in art history, especially miniature and body, and Nur Koçak's photorealist paintings, even if they did not identify as feminists in those years directly. Taner Ceylan's paintings and *Monte Carlo Stili [Monte Carlo Style]* performance, Murat Morova's paintings, and Şükran Moral's performances in the 1990s were early attempts in terms of bringing the queer perspective to the front, but the art world was still a male-dominated, cis scene.[3]

These artists offered an unforgettable rebellion; traditional art education was not enough for them. Artists were seeking more diverse approaches to creation. Hafriyat Group and other initiatives shaped the art world of Istanbul during the 2000s. "Makul & İsyan"

3 "The World Has Become Irrepresentable: A Stroll in the History of Painting", Rana Kelleci - Furkan Öztekin, Painting Today, exhibition catalogue, Ed. Fisun Yalçınkaya, 2024, Istanbul: YKY.

("Reason & Rebellion") (2009), opened by the Hafriyat Group, and "Onur" ("Pride") (2010) were the first exhibitions of the Pride Week in İstanbul. These exhibitions brought new approaches to challenge heteronormativity and bring queer expressions to the scene.

Problematic nature of national identity was at the center of aesthetic discussions. Criticizing current politics was the main issue of Turkey and Turkey's art scene in Istanbul. The art scene was edgy. Kaya Genç explains:

> Contemporary art no longer receives the same attention from Turkey's mainstream publications compared to 2007. Yet the reason for the intense interest in 2007 had a lot to do with the politics of contemporary art of that era. There were subjects that the popular culture industry had considered taboo. Contemporary artists tackled those courageously and were getting into trouble for that. They garnered a reputation for being enfants terribles in the process. After all, they were taking risks on our behalf. They were having a trial by fire while building their careers. And that was something inspiring in that endeavor.

In the contemporary art world of Istanbul, political art hasn't entirely left but there was more crafts, paintings, and handmade sculptures. Genç continues:

> Today it seems significant to me that artists like Yasemin Özcan and İrem Tok have replaced the type of maestro artist that emerged in those years and who outsourced the production of their artworks to artisans. Artists today focus on how they engage with their works rather than explaining how their works should be interpreted.[4]

---

4 "Sanat Eleştirisi ve Gazeteciliği Notları" ["Notes on Art Criticism and Art Journalism"], Kaya Genç, *Sanat Dünyamız* 200, May June Issue, 2024, İstanbul: YKY.

There is a gap in Turkey's written art history about queer-feminist artists. I could only write about the queer exhibitions at the end of the 2000s; to mention queer and feminist artists, I have to rewrite the art history. We know they exist, however, and their works are waiting for us to create the bonds between them. As one of the greatest historians, Reşad Ekrem Koçu, showed us, we can dream of the past and find our queer friends in history.[5] The connections of aesthetics bring us to a place where we dare to do all these. Going back to the techniques of the past in a performative way opens exploring aesthetics from a new perspective.

Artistic expression in contemporary art in Turkey focuses more and more on saving lives, celebrating existence, visibility, and being heard. It is more and more queer. As we say in the local slang, the art scene is now "zırıl."[6] The queer movement feeds on creative expression, and this is an important step in our solidarity. Looking at today's artists who produce with their hands is useful in establishing historical connections and analyzing the aesthetic impact.

As Susan Stryker wrote, "History is not the past. History is a story we tell in the present, one that reaches back to join what can be known of what has already transpired to our vision of whatever yet may come."[7]

---

5 Reşad Ekrem Koçu was a Turkish historian and writer who lived between 1905 and 1975. He wrote an Istanbul Encyclopedia, which tells stories about Istanbul and the people who live there. He opened a unique way into history; as Ezgi Sarıtaş explains in her book, he found friends for himself in history. Ezgi Sarıtaş, Cinsel Normalliğin Kuruluşu: Osmanlı'dan Cumhuriyet'e Heteronormatiflik ve İstikrarsızlıkları [The Establishment of Sexual Normalcy: Heteronormativity and Its Instabilities from the Ottoman Empire to the Republic], İstanbul: Metis Publishing, 2020.

6 Means "full of queer expressions and gestures, shining and shaking with them." This term originally meant "blaring" in Turkish, but here I used it as it belongs to the slang Lubunca, which implies mostly for the queers who came out recently or were just horny or just especially fancy that day. Lubunca is a slang language between queer people made up originally by trans sex workers to protect themselves with secret words talking in between. It's proper not to use it much in order to protect the main purpose of this slang.

7 "On Groundlessness: Transphobic Feminism, Gender Ideology, Transfeminist Critique", Susan Stryker, *Sinistor Wisdom* 128: *Trans/Feminisms*, Spring 2023.

Hands

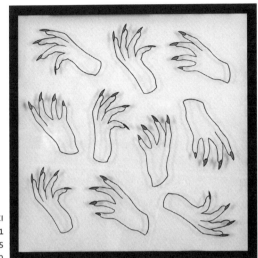

Şafak Şule Kemancı
Ayol hands, 2021
Reverse glass
painting 50x50 cm

Şafak Şule Kemancı
Untitled, 2022
Polymer clay, 20x32 cm

Şafak Şule Kemancı
Untitled, 2021
Fabric, mix medium, 180x90 cm

Interdisciplinary artist and educator Şafak Şule Kemancı is based in Istanbul. They have been a part of the queer activist/artist-run curatorial team called Border/less since 2019. After studying textile design at Central Saint Martin's College of Art and Design in England between 1998 and 2001, Şafak Şule Kemancı studied complementary-functional medicine, and her first works in Istanbul were exhibited in group exhibitions at Karşı Sanat Çalışmaları,

Tüyap Art Fair, Teşvikiye Art Gallery, and Hisart between 2003 and 2005. Following these, the artist studied art at Goldsmiths University of London for her master's degree between 2006 and 2008.

It's not easy to summarize the art life of Şafak with their education. They have a long history of opening solo exhibitions, participating in group exhibitions with their works, collaborating with artists, and organizing the last Pride Week exhibitions in Istanbul.

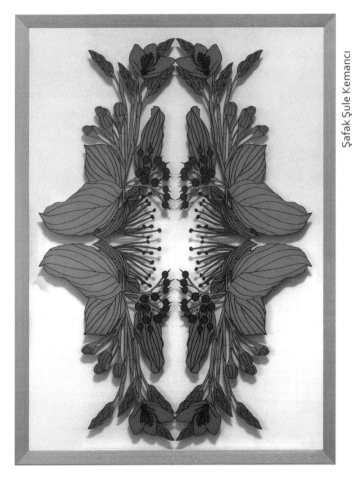

Şafak Şule Kemancı
Untitled Vulva series, 2021
Reverse glass painting, 50x70 cm

Among these, they have created a world that's only their own, with glitter, velvet, and fur and patterns including love, growing, and sex evolving. To me, Cecilia Alemani's definition of Leonora

Carrington's world is accurate for Şafak as well: "It's a world where everyone can change, be transformed, become something or someone else; a world set free, brimming with possibilities." Şafak says that sometimes they feel closer to plants than to people. And in their creation in the last decade, anything you see is half human, half plant, or a connection between plants and people.

Their work, *Ayol Eller* [Ayol Hands], is not different. They create a hand gesture painted on glass with black or gold lines and lots of glitter. They say that the glitter is a part of queer culture, just like magic. *Ayol Eller* [Ayol Hands] is a representation of a claw-out figure. But these hands only have four fingers; therefore, they seem human, but they don't belong to humans. They're strong and threatening. Just like *Ayol Eller* [Ayol Hands], the artist's big and soft fabric sculptures *Untitled I–II* (2021) (measured 180 x 90 x 90 cm and 220 x 60 x 60 cm and exhibited in Şafak's solo show in Depo Istanbul titled "All the birds would come to my garden") make the audience feel like they can touch and hug them; they seem full of compassion, but if you get too close, they can be dangerous, just like the carnivorous plants. On the opposite of them, Şafak's small sculptures resemble the clitoris' and are exhibited inside the bell jars. They seem so fragile that the audience feels like it's not safe to touch them; they may break into pieces so easily, but through their leaves again, they imply that they're hiding something playful and dangerous. It makes the audience think that maybe that's why they're captured in those jars in the first place. They all involve hand gestures similar to *Ayol Eller* [Ayol Hands]. You can see the nails and limbs if you closely look at them without getting bitten, if you can.

Şafak talks about plants' role in their art, saying, "They're big; they say that they can bite you; they can do what they want; they're strong, but I don't define them with the word 'bold'. They don't owe anyone to be brave, nice, or normal. We don't owe anyone to be brave either. As lesbians and queers, we don't owe anyone to be nice. My works seem colorful and playful, but when you contact them deeply, one can see that they're not so innocent; they involve magic in them, the power to transform the elements of the world. They're doing so by just being, existing, and showing themselves as they are."[8]

Okyanus Çağrı Çamcı. I never promised you a rose garden, 2023
Water color on paper, 24x18 cm

Through this mischievous world, I move to the art of Okyanus Çağrı Çamcı. Okyanus is an artist based in İzmir and partly in Istan-

---

8 From the conversation with the artist, dated 9 April 2024.

bul. She graduated from Dokuz Eylül University in 2022, having studied painting. Her works are a combination of watercolor, oil, and different techniques of painting. She combines stories about gender, family, sense of belonging, and struggles of life. She says, "I want to show what's hidden. I want to show the feelings that are not on the surface. What motivates me is the urge to open a locked box. One of my paintings shows a trans child on a birthday. The child should be happy; however, there's something wrong with the room as well; there's something hidden. Or, as in one other painting, a bride on her wedding day, for example. She should be happy, but squeezed between her big brother and her new husband, she's repressed and far away from happiness. It's hard for me to see through everything that is going on with her, but it becomes easier when I try to feel it through the painting."[9]

The hands of that bride in the painting called *Ortaklık* [Partnership] (pencil and water color on paper, 40 x 30 cm, 2023, exhibited in the exhibition called "Resurgence in Fragments") were the first I saw of Okyanus's works, and they stayed in my mind with their

9 From the conversation with the artist, dated 14 March 2024.

Okyanus Çağrı Çamcı. Partnership, 2023
Pencil and water color on paper, 40x30 cm

closed gesture. This elegant hand gesture is an expression of kindness and grace among young women. But there is something hidden in it. Maybe these are the hands that meet to cover a wound. She paints this with the inspiration of her own mother's wedding picture. She explains in the article she wrote for the exhibition catalog of "Resurgence in Fragments":

My mother looks at me like a prisoner in handcuffs from her wedding photo. This feeling is very familiar to me, like trying to hold a barbed wire with both hands. The account book left by my father is full of successive lists of receivables and payables. It is covered with the paper of a famous cartoon of the period. I think about what the hand-knitted rose that my brother sent from prison tells me; I witness the gender norms, responsibilities, and economic difficulties imposed on my mother, father, and older brother. Knowing that it may not be possible to embrace our assigned family, I hope that we will find peace with our chosen families.[10]

10 Exhibition catalog of "Resurgence in Fragments," held between 16 June – 5 August 2023, in Depo Istanbul.

The roses in Okyanus's painting have a special place as well. In her painting titled *Sana Gül Bahçesi Vadetmedim* [I never promised you a rose garden] (water color on paper, 24 x 18 cm, 2023, exhibited in the exhibition called "Resurgence in Fragments"), she showed a painting of a pink rose right next to the *Ortaklık* [Partnership]. The color of the rose seems like a wound on a woman's body. Maybe the hands meet to close a wound, and if the rose is coming from the same point as the wound, could the healing needed come from the rose? Could this be a transformation of closing then opening? Maybe the hands closed just to open again. When they are open, the rose, painted in the color of the wound, arises, demonstrating the continuation of life, healing, and connecting with the past. One Alevi folk song in Turkish, *Gül Türküsü* [Song of Roses], reminds me of a surreal painting where everything turns into roses. The roses are both the ones that weigh and are weighed and those that measure and are measured, and the ones that sell these roses are roses as well.[11] There is no other point of value or being other than being a rose leaf, which is one of the lightest things in the world. With the inspiration of this song, the artist turns into a rose as well.

A similarity to the hands of that bride comes across again with the artist's new series *Bu Sana Hoşçakal Demek* [This Means Goodbye to You] (pastel and spray on paper, triptych, each 50 x 50 cm, 2024, exhibited in the exhibition called Trauma Response, held between 6th and 11th of May, 2024, at Tayyare Cultural Center). In this black and white triptych, hands on the stomach, the core of the body, come together or set apart. First, close, and then open, or the reverse. Okyanus shows the process this time, with all the surviving inspirations in it.

---

11 The song goes like, "Buying the roses, selling the roses, they held a scale made of roses; the ones who buy are roses, the ones who sell as weel." (Gül alırlar, gül satarlar, gülden terazi tutarlar, alanlar gül satanlar gül) (Song is anonymous; translation belongs to the writer.)

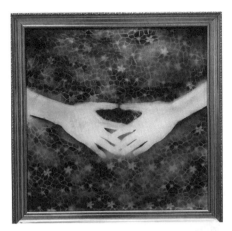

Okyanus Çağrı Çamcı
This means goodbye to you, 2024
Pastel and spray on paper, triptych
Each 50x50 cm

Stomach

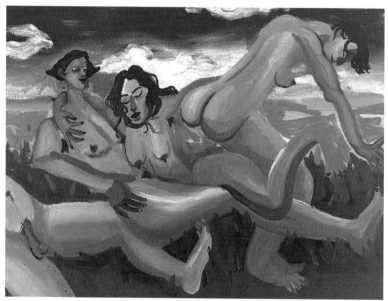

Yaz Taşçı. Everywhere's dizzy, 2021. Oil on canvas, 30×50 cm

Yaz Taşçı. İkindi [Noon], 2021. Rapido on paper, 35×50

Yaz Taşçı, Made it look better than it is, 2022.
Mixed media on canvas, 94×180 cm, 2022

was born in a small city on the Black Sea coast of Turkey, Sinop. She lives in Istanbul and is currently in Paris for the prestigious residency program at Cité Internationale des Arts Paris. Yaz is an artist who painted the sky orange when she was a child, and maybe she noticed how she liked to play with shades and change the sky right at that age. In her paintings such as *Olduğundan Daha Güzel Göstermiş* [better than it is] (oil on canvas, 94 x 180 cm, 2022) what strikes first is the change in the shades of color of the naked bodies: from the pale pinks to the shades of purple, from the reds to the green, yellow, and blue. The colors combine with the actions of the figures in the paintings. Figures that look at a painting, play *tavla* [backgammon], make love, swim, or just stand in the sea, touching each other, and mostly, as in the most effective way, look at the audience in the eye from a bizarre heaven. This aesthetic gesture of looking into the eye again comes from the core of the body. The big, round, or muscle bellies in her paintings seem like they found happiness and joy in a place that is not so far from our land as in the painting *Heryer Dönüyor* (Oil on canvas, 30 x 50 cm, 2021).

Yaz Taşçı studied fine arts in high school and then ceramics at the university, but, after a while, she left the academy and became a self-taught painter who also learned from artists around her and from the environment. She defines herself as a young Lubunya (the word in Lubunca for queer) who came to Istanbul to get involved in the activism circles in this city and now has a great group of friends. Therefore, she says that she thought at first that she painted those around herself, and therefore she painted small figures in a big land like in the painting *İkindi* [Noon] (Ink on paper, 30 x 42.5 cm, 2019), where all of them seem like one big shape. As time went by, her figures started growing, and the land started shrinking. Now she says that for all this time, by painting her figures while thinking she is painting friends and lovers, she actually paints herself. This way of looking comes from her own art. One learns from the subconscious through one's own paintings. This story is the story of all of us; it is our story.

This mutual story resonates with Şafak Şule Kemancı's series of reverse glass vulvas (dated 2021, each 50 x 70 cm). This is a series of vulvas turning into plants. For this series, Şafak asked friends to take a picture of their vulvas and in the work they used the exact same color of the vulvas. When we talk about these series, they say, "This was actually about others, but it was about me, to tell my story and to exist."[12]

Roots

Şafak says Istanbul is the city where she fell on her back in a concert and the crowd held her in their hands; this crowd is the writers, artists, and friends in Istanbul.

Yaz says about her paintings and Istanbul:

> These are my alternative worlds, my paradises. Sometimes I wonder if this place has become a place of unrealistic fantasies. I also think that I am speaking for many people who suffer from similar problems. We all establish contact from the moment we are born, and

---

12 From the conversation with the artist, 9 April 2024.

*as long as this contact is in a safe space, it's good. I
think that I have established my safe space in Istanbul
in a sincere, warm, and caring way. I cannot do some
things, but I have close friends who know that I cannot do these things, and they do those for me, and I do
what falls on my part.[13]*

Journalist Hazal Sipahi asked Okyanus in a video interview program "Ayrık Otu" [Weed Grass] on T24 how it is to be apart from
the cis, male-centered art world of Istanbul and be based in İzmir
as a trans artist. Okyanus responded, "My story began in Gire-
sun among women artists and continued in İzmir with solidarity.
I started talking too late. In my early memories, I spoke with my
hands. In İzmir, I was drawn to people who understood me. But to
be seen as queers in İzmir was quite hard; some collectives such as
Darağaç opened their doors, but these examples are limited. So, I
need Istanbul."

Istanbul has a connection with the long-term struggles of the
artists of Turkey: the dilemma of being away (in the periphery?)
or being in the center. Yaz, Şafak, and Okyanus were nurtured by
the art history that has yet to be written. Their techniques show us
how to find bonds in the archive today and in the future.

The theme of the 32nd Istanbul Pride Week in 2024 is "I remember; do you remember?" These connections are magical. Connecting with the past is our right and our need. We want to remember
and celebrate the anniversaries of the big, crowded pride marches in 2013 and 2014. More than that, we want to remember the
future; with roses, shiny plants, and eyes looking at us from the
most beautiful heaven we can ever imagine, with an orange sky
and bodies in every color. This is the power of the queer aesthetic
in Istanbul; it means demanding lives, demanding performativity,
and demanding existence.

---

13   From the conversation with the artist, 19 March, 2024.

COVER ARTIST STATEMENT

Kinga Stefaniec

I explore alternative contemplations looking answers how to manage survival in existential crisis I research subjects in theory formulate alchemy in gold consistency cosmic intelligence house planetary set up concentration on communication pressurizing urges to explain reason this old pirate town made overthink subjects in theory and experimental curiosity explaining results over molecules fusion on perception subject to experimentations expanding insight on interpretation bending access through back doors projector of Reality. Implanted in alternative City & Town scene decorations Turbo Island as psycholocation with high rezonation reason nations qualities projection through imprints on mental experimental simulation script plays interactive city game projections focusing on street level where society is coexisting in perspectives allowed to see the City alternative Peoples Republic of Stokes Croft planted on plot of no man's land. Turbo Island burn campfire in the town. Fire burn for fifteen years nearly all the time. Firewatch regulate the traffic of the street in hot debates patchwork toxic patterns and healing exchange feelings and gather in expanding community concrete jungle I walk everyday seeing new details of changing times.

I see in overseer role play game storyline engaging to translate state of mind universum sucking inside station Locoation to watch the street which never sleeps in the social context coexist on mental map navigations search pirates gold with precision excavate layers on top of each other constructed sacred geometry in hallucinations decode signatures water trademarks in observations impressions in psychoactive game this town play on oldschool tapes.

I explore writing down uncounsciouss streaming communication sequences explaining Animatrix experimental language I called Kinglish to make reader aware that its creative reinvented poetic narrative modify reportage simultanusly copy realismatic time travel in upgraded version Gonzo style influences bringing its origin in polishing accent breaking free from restrictions setup by ignoring stiffed regulations grammar gramatures breaks golden rules inflicting cyberpunk in creatively reinvented streaming automatic writing CodeX annihilated political context in artistic future primitive community dealing settled around the fire to discuss inflammable derogatory topics fighting prejudice and stereotypes. Broken language dyslectic aversion in communication breakdown reconnecting contrculture sends inspirations in multicultural town I found networks connections supporting original Vision follow up Neo Beat Generation sacrum profanum artistic experimenting role serving the artist in outcast avoidance feed creativity to beat spleen through spliff dealing mental episodes induced by turbulent relationships bringing risky psychotic insight into environmental transgression Neo bitniks transplanted mental change in activation as conterculture in progressed timescales relocoations fixated on molecules resources transfers in laser hologram sealing mystic visionary inspirations in poetic interpretation crossing personal Jesus second coming to Turbo Island where wooden pallets build the stake in flames serving warm up modern witches romanticized South West smoking dope selling junk Interzona takes over Naked Lunch reality instant scenery overrun score instant cravings hunger sucking souls in ramblings through the intervals timing schedule regular urges romance smoking progrow in earthly village relocated here from everywhere craving quick fix on the streets recovering minds of my generation howl!

Street reprogram superman conscioussnes in Hive overlooking the cosmic tunnel of human soul connected to the source in mystic hallucinations build mythic United Kingadom installed as feminine secret king on exile writing scripts in tribal mode connections relations. As ethical junkies free spirit in the reject drop out on the dole can retreat to be in idealistic pure existential engaged artist as Neo bitniks courious souls imprisoned poisoned terminated criticized in outdated system malfunction detection fatal error disabled progress in simulation I research antidotum to fix the glitch computer generated randomisator in cut up techniques improvisator creator spelling realistic magic power as wordsmith shooting weapon in words as swords ink drinking weapon I master my pen Bob all mighty symbol my Excalibur in review my name rewrited feminine King claimed diesel dyke on heroine journey lifetime quest to find Holy Grail in remission symptoms I realized true purpose as poet inspired by Fire Goddess deliver holy script in universal codex reprogramming installation unlocking superpowers hidden in serpents DNA.

In black sheep's flock of souls reincarnated instant location topic in hedonism consumerism disposal society make profits in contrast future primitive tribal symbiosis contrculture write recipes how to fix that loop hole leaking default in expired operative system malfunctions. I got to outline computerised animatrix vocabulary in RPG simulations first person point of view reporter who describe the mistic experiences with substances changing perception insight to change the game rules in anxious times when we are not sure how to cope on slippery slope.

I am depraved dreams since forced intoxication on prescribed medications suppressing psyche but still in autotherapy this animation is automaticon register in rebellious town covered in graffitti the awareness witnessing registry in non binary code personality bios settings programming computer animated algorithm calculations mathematic quotation summarise in keyword sequences translations how to fix the loophole endangers freezing psychoactive key opening mystery lock to dig stored data in crystal cave hidden in depths of human mind micro universe reflection in ancient mystic contradictions of reality detachments reordering chaos of times under threatening military actions in micro scale debates raising awareness in subcultural context alternative reality reorganizing societal norms induced by engaged figures who inspire the minds who crave warm relationships which help to

shake the desease humanity repetitive self destructitive tendencies will transform interpretation in decoded DNA key unlocking
god mode locked secrets interpretations fatum that hounting un-
certainty in our human species cosmic identity lighting up track to
find resolution existential mystery humans discover cosmic identity searching true destiny.

CONTRIBUTOR NOTES

Aviva Betzer is a graduate student in the Department of English Literature and American Studies at Tel Aviv University. She is writing her thesis on the double in Sylvia Plath's poetry. She majored with honors in the studies of Theory of Literature at Tel Aviv University, focusing on the representations of the Freudian body in the fiction of David Vogel. Her work has been published in *Caesura*, *Chambers Anthology*, *Arc* and *The Foundationalist* and is forthcoming in *Mantis*.

Cassandra Langer graduated from NYU with a doctorate in critical studies and art history, is a Smithsonian postdoctoral fellow, author of 10 books and taught at FIU, USC, Hunter, and Queens College. She has written for Arts, College Art Journal, Art Papers, Woman's Art Journal, Ms. Magazine, Women's Review of Books, New York Newsday Sinister Wisdom and The Gay and Lesbian Review Worldwide. Dr. Langer has lectured widely and is the 21st century another of Romaine Brooks: A Life. Her latest Book is Erase Her: A Survivors Story. She is currently work on My Gay Miami 1960-1979.

Cassidy Hunt is a recent graduate from the University of Edinburgh where she studied Philosophy and Politics as an undergraduate. She has been volunteering with Sinister Wisdom since summer 2023 and has a love for all things related to lesbian archiving, history and culture!

C. LaSandra Cummings is a multi-genre writer from Orlando, Florida. She earned her BA and MA from the University of Central Florida; and earned an MFA in Creative Writing from the University of Colorado at Boulder, where she was awarded the *Jovanovich Imaginative Writing Award* and a *"Best Should Teach" Silver Award*.

Her poetry appears in *Obsidian, African American Review,* and elsewhere. Her scholarship appears in *Callaloo.* She works as an educator and writing coach.

Cris Hernández is a Butch-Chicana-Lesbian-Feminist, in no particular order except as determined by context. With a BA in History and a minor in Women's Studies (because they didn't have a major yet) from Cal State Long Beach, poetry became a better medium for writing her analysis of the world around her rather than research papers. Her poems have appeared in: *The Lodestar Quarterly, The Peralta Press, The Blue Mouse, Las Girlfriends, Jota, and Saga.* She is currently working on a second chapbook tentatively titled *Pilgrimage Home,* constructing and interrogating shifting identities over time. Her first chapbook, *Un Corazón Inquieto,* is available by contacting Cris at: crowhawkarts@gmail.com. Cris has also read and hosted poetry readings at numerous venues in Southern California. Cris lives with her wife of over twenty years in Long Beach, CA. They are joined by Harley who is, of course, a tortoise shell cat.

Dakota Sebourn is a professional photographer from the PNW. Her art is her ritual, she seeks to create in harmony with the magic of the world, be it in the studio or a serendipitous encounter in the wild. She creates her photographs on 35mm, 120, 127, and 4x5 film, developed herself. Her work has been featured in exhibits with Slip Gallery, Photocenter of the North West, and Sari Sari Studios, in addition to various publications including "WMN Zine", "Lesbians are Miracles", and "Beyond the Veil Press". You can see more of her art on her website, www.seawitch.photography.

Dartricia Rollins is a Queer, Black, Southern organizer, memory worker, and cultural worker. Dartricia's latest project is Georgia Dusk: a southern liberation oral history project connecting the intersections of Black movement and cultural work in Atlanta, Georgia across generations.

Demetria Martinez is a writer, poet, and immigrant rights activist known for engaging with spiritual, transformative, and political themes in her writing. Her work includes the award-winning *Mother Tongue*, based partly on her experience as a reporter being indicted and acquitted on First Amendment grounds for assisting Central American refugees, her essay collection, *Confessions of a Berlitz-Tape Chicana*, which won the International Latino Book Award, and poetry collections titled *The Devil's Workshop* (2002), *Breathing Between the Lines* (1997), *and Turning* (1987). She collaboratively authored "These People Want to Work: Immigration Reform" (2013), which portrays the struggles of undocumented women in the U.S. and analyzes immigration reform. She was awarded the Luis Leal Award for Distinction in Chicano/Latino Literature.

EJ Hicks (they/he) is a butch dyke and English professor living in Illinois with their fiancée and their dog, Hobie. When they're not teaching composition classes, they read, crochet, and attempt to garden. They mainly write about queerness, monsters, nature, and the body; their work has been published in Eastern Illinois University's literary journal The Vehicle (Spring 2023) and Rising Phoenix Press (October 2023). You can find them on Instagram at @emrysjamespoetry or wherever yarn is sold. This poem is dedicated to their fiancée.

Fisun Yalçınkaya, born in Istanbul, is a journalist and art writer. From 2009 to 2019, they reported for various daily and weekly newspapers and worked as editors. Since 2019, Fisun has been the editor-in-chief of an art magazine and contributes to several art publications. Also they have been organizing monthly independent workshops since 2023. These workshops focus on contemporary art and creative protests, fostering a vibrant community of female artists and activists.

Gale P. Jackson is a passionate embracer of language, poetry, and storytelling. She was raised amidst the transformative influence of narrative, cultural richness, and the enchantment of art, and her life's dedication unfolds as a deep engagement with learning and community building. She is the author of *Suite for Mozambique* (2006), *MeDea* (2001), *Bridge Suite: Narrative Poems* (1998), *Khoisan Tale of Beginnings & Ends* (1998), and "We Stand Our Ground" (1988) with Kimiko Hahn and Susan Sherman. With a focus on feminism, African studies, humanism, and generalism, she continues to explore the potential within each pedagogical space and contribute to the pursuit of a just world.

Jan Clausen is a poet, writer, and educator renowned for her insightful explorations of identity and social justice issues through various literary forms. In the 1970s, she co-founded the journal *Conditions* as a "magazine of writing by women with an emphasis on writing by lesbians." Her work includes poetry, fiction, essays, and the memoir *Apples & Oranges: My Journey through Sexual Identity* (first published in 1999 and reissued with a new introduction by Seven Stories Press in 2017). Her most recent poetry collection is *Veiled Spill: A Sequence* (GenPop Books, 2014). Her fiction titles focused on lesbian experience include the story collection *Mother, Sister, Daughter, Lover* and the novel *Sinking, Stealing*, a story about lesbian coparenting in the days before such relationships could be legally protected.

Kara Olson is a poet and educator. She is a graduate of Warren Wilson's MFA Program for Writers, a recipient of a Jerome Foundation-supported residency at the Anderson Center, and a member of the Queer Voices writing circles in collaboration with Hennepin County and Quatrefoil Library. Her poem "Last Night" was selected by Donika Kelly as winner of *The Sewanee Review's* annual Poetry Contest. Additional poems appear in *Grist: A Journal of The Literary Arts*, *Waterstone Review*, and elsewhere. She lives in Minneapolis and is a professor of English at North Hennepin Community College where she is humbled daily by working with students from all walks of life and by advocating for educational equity and justice.

Kit Kennedy is a queer elder, poet, blogger and photographer living in Walnut Creek, CA. She has published seven collections, including *while eating oysters* (CLWN WR BKS, Brooklyn, NY). Work has appeared in Sinister Wisdom, Tipton Poetry Journal, Great Weather for Media, First Literary Review-East, Gyroscope, Shot Glass Journal, and California Quarterly. She serves as Poet-in-Residence of the San Francisco Bay Times and Resident Poet at Ebenezer Lutheran "herchurch." Please visit: https://poetrybites.blogspot.com.

L.A. "Happy" Hyder likes the term 'artivist' to define her years as a visual artist, writer, founder/director LVA: Lesbians in the Visual Arts (1990-2003), curator, and dancer. She says, "This is the first I've shared these images of Audre. I looked at them recently, found out Audre would have been 90 in 2024, and approached *Sinister Wisdom* as the place for them." Hyder, now living in Mendocino CA, is grateful every day for where her path has taken her. She can be reached at lahyderphotography@gmail.com.

Maida Tilchen is a writer and book collector. Since 1993, she has been writing historical novels about lesbians in New Mexico in the 1920s. Her 2009 novel *Land Beyond Maps* was a Lammy Finalist 2010 for Lesbian Debut Fiction and a Golden Crown Literary Society 2010 Finalist for Dramatic/General Fiction. Her second novel *She's Gone Santa Fe* was a Golden Crown Literary Society "Goldie" Award Finalist 2014 for Historical Fiction. Her adventures collecting New Mexico books were featured in *New Mexico Magazine* (January, 2020) and her New Mexico collection won the 2020 Ticknor Society Book Collecting Prize. In 2025, the Lilly Library, a rare book library in Bloomington, Indiana, acquired Maida's entire collection of lesbian pulp novels, lesbian periodicals, and lesbian ephemera. It will be available for today's students, researchers, and the general public.

Margaret Randall is a poet, feminist, photographer, oral historian, and social activist with more than 200 works to her name. She co-founded the bilingual journal *El Corno Emplumado/The Plumed Horn*. She actively participated in the 1968 Mexican student movement and, when forced to flee, was led to Cuba, where she resided for 11 years. "To Change the World: My Years in Cuba" (2009) reflects on her time there. Later, living in Nicaragua, she explored the intersection of socialist revolutionary societies and feminism in her work. Upon return to the U.S., she faced deportation, but after a five-year legal battle, she was successful, earning further recognition for her writing and human rights activism.

Mary Maxfield (they/ she) uses nonfiction, poetry, fiction, and research to explore queerness, healing, and community. Their past publications include *Catapult*, *Strange Horizons*, and *Sweeter Voices Still: An LGBTQ Anthology from Middle America*. Mary has been honored as a Lambda Literary Fellow and a finalist in Button Poetry's annual spoken-word contest. Find her online at marymaxfield.com.

Maureen C. (Cullingham) lives in Ottawa, Ontario, Canada, and has collected vintage lesbian novels since the mid-1970s.

René Baek Goddard started her career as a news reporter for KUAR Public Radio and Arkansas Public Media. Her work has appeared in Truthout, Autostraddle, and the Arkansas Worker. She has over five years of social justice organizing experience, and is currently incarcerated for charges related to the 2020 George Floyd uprisings.

Roberta Arnold is a lop-sided lesbian elder living in the mountains of Southwest Virginia. She is very close, physically and mentally, to her sister, dog, and cat. And as the song goes: *none of whom truly belongs to me*. She walks and swims and reads and writes and find herself daily in awe of nature and animals. She was born in

Houston and raised in New York City and has done a good bit of seeing the world. In her good fortune, she was born into a world spurred on by a most unusual and innovative lesbian feminist writer mother, June Arnold. She has published stories and book reviews in *Sinister Wisdom: A Multicultural Lesbian Literary & Art Journal*. Back in the 70s, she sat down on a grassy lawn and wrote a short story for *Ain't I A Woman? Press* in Iowa City, Iowa, when traveling across the country with a van full of radical dykes. This journey was outlined by her and her outlaw compadres in *Sinister Wisdom 89: Reconciliations*. More recently, she had a book review about Andrea Dworkin in *Ms*. She volunteers and served on the board at *Sinister Wisdom*. She is a member of Dykewriters and OLOC.

Robin Cohen (Rob Ceeme on Facebook) sees no reason to boast her CV, former art, honors, accomplishments as she is now a happily retired snowbird and traveler who welcomes new travel mates and continues to welcome any academic or grassroots opportunities to present from or share her vast lesbian pulps knowledge and perspectives.

Ronna Magy is a poet and memoirist. Recently honored by West Hollywood as a civil rights hero, Ronna has curated readings of senior queer women poets for Circa: Queer Histories Festival, the LA LGBT Center, and Outwrite. In 2023 she participated in the Napa Valley Writers Conference. Her poetry appears in *Rise Up Review, The Los Angeles Press, Wild Crone Wisdom, Poetry Super Highway, Persimmon Tree, Writing in a Woman's Voice, Writers Resist,* and *Nasty Women Poets*. She's a subject matter expert in teaching English as a Second Language and textbook author.

Ruth Dworin lives in Toronto, where she does book-keeping and financial management for arts organizations, publishers, and arts related small businesses. From 1980 to 1990, she produced women's music, theatre, dance and comedy as the Artistic Director of Womynly Way Productions and sat on the founding Board of AWMAC (Association of Women's Music and Culture).

Samantha Nye graduated from the School of the Museum of Fine Arts at Tufts University and received an SMFA traveling fellowship. Her fellowship enabled her to go to Italy, where she researched Italian cinema and queer communities. She won a prestigious Guggenheim in 2022, and her work has been exhibited at the Museum of Fine Arts in Boston, Candice Madey Gallery, The Armory Show, and featured in Art Forum and Hyperallergic.

Dr. Shariananda Adamz has worked in religious spaces and the arts since the 1990s as an author, healer, life coach, theater artist, social worker, practitioner of reiki, and more. The founder of Woman in the Moon Publications, Adamz's writing has been published by several presses, including Simon & Schuster and Sinister Wisdom. In addition to writing, Adamz teaches workshops on spirituality and healing. Through this work, she aims to be a spiritual guide and counselor for those who need it.

Susan Sherman is a founding editor of *IKON* magazine, as well as the source of life for its Second Series, which she revived in 1982 and ran until 1994. She is also an avid and award-winning writer, poet, and playwright. She's published seven poetry collections, an essay and short fiction collection, a memoir, and twelve off-off Broadway shows. Her latest book, *The Light that Puts an End to Dreams* (Wings Press, 2012), is an autobiography conveyed through poetry and prose and documents her involvement with critical events of our time. Sherman's work has never shied from challenging existing norms and ideas of love, activism, change, and freedom.

Suzanne DeWitt Hall (she/they) is the author of THE LANGUAGE OF BODIES, which Wally Lamb called "...a film noir between covers—dark, tense, and sexy." Other books include Where True Love Is devotionals, the Living in Hope series which supports family and friends of transgender people, The Path of Unlearning faith deconstruction books, and the Rumplepimple adventures. Their poetry has been included in a variety of anthologies.

Tate is an ODU graduate of Creative Writing. Her internationally-recognized, prize-winning work is featured or forthcoming in the Mace & Crown, Tealight Press, Anti-Heroin Chic, Bitchin' Kitsch, Oddball Magazine, Other Worldly Women, Lovers Literary Journal, Pretty Progressive, Tipping the Scales, Bullshit Lit, and Never Sent Zine. She currently lives in Nashville with her fiancé and author, Marissa LaRocca.

Vagia Kalfa (they/ them) is a PhD candidate at the Amsterdam School of Cultural Analysis. They have published the poetic collections Απλά Πράγματα (Gavrielides, 2012) and Μακάρι Να Το Είχα Κάνει Νωρίτερα (Thraka, 2023). Their first collection was awarded the "Y. Athanas Award" by the Academy of Athens and "Y. Varveris Award" by the Hellenic Authors Society. They hold a column in the magazines Thraka and Poeticanet, where they publish essays and reviews with a focus on feminist and LGBTQ+ literature. They have been a co-anthologist in the Anthology of Greek Queer Poetry (Thraka & Rosa Luxemburg Foundation, 2023). They edited poems and short stories on violence against women in a series of issues published by Thraka (December 2023- March 2024) and curated the reading night "Women on Scene", co-hosted by Thraka and the network of women writers against gender-based violence and femicides I Foni tis (March 8, 2024).

Order Sinister Wisdom´s Sapphic Classics

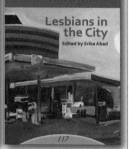